The Complete Healthy Smoothie Recipe Book, Soup Maker Recipe Book, Vegetarian Cookbook & 5 2 Fast Diet

Table of Contents

The Complete Healthy Smoothie Recipe Book

Introduction

If you are tired of carrying around those excess pounds and are seeking ways to feel your best in a colorful, easy way, then smoothies are a perfect go-to!

This book is loaded with over 100 delicious, easy-to-make smoothie recipes that will help you much more than just melting off that weight you wish to lose! From boosting your energy to making your skin more radiant, these smoothie recipes are a foolproof way to get you back on track with your overall health.

While there are tons of smoothie books on the market today, there are none quite like this one! Thank you again for choosing this book. Every effort was made to ensure it is full of as much useful information as possible, please enjoy!

BONUS:

As a way of saying thank you for purchasing my book, please use your link below to claim your 3 FREE Cookbooks on Health, Fitness & Dieting Instantly

https://bit.ly/2OazEZu

You can also share your link with your friends and families whom you think that can benefit from the cookbooks or you can forward them the link as a gift!

At the end of every bundle can you copy and paste this:

** Remember to use your link to claim your 3 FREE Cookbooks on Health, Fitness & Dieting Instantly

https://bit.ly/2OazEZu

Chapter 1: Healthy Heart

Carrot Papaya Protein Smoothie

Ingredients:

- 4 ice cubes
- ½ C. berries of choice
- ¼ C. carrot juice
- 1 scoop of whey protein, your choice of flavor
- ½ papaya

Here's how to do it:

1. Mix everything in a blender.
2. Puree ingredients until smooth in texture or you reach your desired consistency.

Blueberry Avocado Protein Smoothie

Ingredients:

- 4 ice cubes
- ½ an avocado
- 1 C. frozen blueberries
- 1 scoop whey protein, your choice of flavor
- 1 C. coconut water

Here's how to do it:

1. Mix everything in a blender.
2. Puree ingredients until smooth in texture or you reach your desired consistency.

Chia Seed Acai Berry Protein Smoothie

Ingredients:

- 1 scoop whey protein, your choice of flavor
- 2 tbsp. chia seeds
- 3 ounces frozen acai berries
- 2 C. unsweetened almond milk

Here's how to do it:

1. Mix everything in a blender.
2. Puree ingredients until smooth in texture or you reach your desired consistency.

Banana Oat Protein Smoothie

Ingredients:

- 4 ice cubes
- 1 scoop whey protein, your choice of flavor
- 1 tsp. honey
- ¼ tsp. cinnamon
- 1 C. unsweetened almond milk
- 4 tbsp. rolled oats
- 2 bananas

Here's how to do it:

1. Mix everything in a blender.
2. Puree ingredients until smooth in texture or you reach your desired consistency.

Chocolate Peanut Butter Protein Smoothie

Ingredients:

- 1 C. low-fat yogurt
- 1 scoop whey protein, your choice of flavor
- 1 frozen banana
- 2 tbsp. 100% chocolate syrup
- 2 tbsp. peanut butter
- ½ C. low-fat milk

Here's how to do it:

1. Mix everything in a blender.
2. Puree ingredients until smooth in texture or you reach your desired consistency.

Green Flax Smoothie

Ingredients:

- ½ C. frozen pineapple chunks
- 2 C. spinach
- 1 banana
- 2 peeled clementines
- 2 tbsp. flax seeds
- ½ C. water

Here's how to do it:

1. Mix everything in a blender.
2. Puree ingredients until smooth in texture or you reach your desired consistency.

The Healthy Start Smoothie

Ingredients:

- 1 C. ice cubes
- ¾ C. frozen mango chunks
- 1 C. fresh pineapple chunks
- 1 ½ C. kale
- 1 tbsp. agave nectar
- 1 tbsp. chia seeds
- ½ C. low-fat cottage cheese
- 6 ounces water

Here's how to do it:
1. Mix everything in a blender.
2. Puree ingredients until smooth in texture or you reach your desired consistency.

Fudgesicle Frosty Smoothie

Ingredients:

- 3 C. ice cubes
- ½ of a peeled/pitted avocado
- 4 pitted Medjool dates
- 1/3 C. cocoa powder
- ¼ C. agave nectar
- 2/3 C. coconut milk

Here's how to do it:
1.   Mix everything in a blender.
2.   Puree ingredients until smooth in texture or you reach your desired consistency.

Orange Julicious Smoothie

Ingredients:

- 1 tsp. vanilla extract
- 2 tbsp. honey
- 6 ounces frozen orange juice concentrate
- 1 ½ C. ice cubes
- 1 C. yellow squash
- 2 peeled oranges
- 1 C. low-fat milk

Here's how to do it:

1. Mix everything in a blender.
2. Puree ingredients until smooth in texture or you reach your desired consistency.

Green Monster Smoothie

Ingredients:

- 1 C. ice cubes
- 1 C. frozen mango
- 1 C. spinach
- 1 C. kale
- ½ banana
- 1 cored/quartered apple of choice
- 12 ounces orange juice

Here's how to do it:

1. Mix everything in a blender.
2. Puree ingredients until smooth in texture or you reach your desired consistency.

Red Rose Lemonade Smoothie

Ingredients:

- 1 C. ice
- 1 C. water
- 1 tsp. rose hips powder
- ½ an inch of ginger
- ½ juiced lemon
- 1 chopped apple of choice
- 4 ounces chopped beets

Here's how to do it:

1. Mix everything in a blender.
2. Puree ingredients until smooth in texture or you reach your desired consistency.

Fine-Apple Smoothie

Ingredients:

- 1 C. ice
- 1 C. water
- 3 tbsp. cashews
- 1 tbsp. yacon root
- 4 ounces cantaloupe
- 4 ounces pineapple
- 4 ounces grapes

Here's how to do it:

1. Mix everything in a blender.
2. Puree ingredients until smooth in texture or you reach your desired consistency.

"The Kiwi to My Heart" Smoothie

Ingredients:

- 1 C. ice
- 1 C. water
- 1 tbsp. hemp seeds
- 1 juiced lime
- 1 chopped cucumber
- 1 peeled kiwi
- 1 chopped pear
- 1 ½ ounces baby spinach

Here's how to do it:
1. Mix everything in a blender.
2. Puree ingredients until smooth in texture or you reach your desired consistency.

Spiced Orange Cider Smoothie

Ingredients:

- 1 C. ice
- 1 C. water
- ¼ tsp. ground cloves
- 1 tbsp. pea protein
- ½ juiced lemon
- 1 tbsp. apple cider vinegar
- ½ pitted avocado
- 2 peeled clementines
- 1 ½ ounces collard greens

Here's how to do it:

1. Mix everything in a blender.

2. Puree ingredients until smooth in texture or you reach your desired consistency.

Chocolate Covered Coconut Smoothie

Ingredients:

- 1 C. ice
- 1 C. coconut water
- 2 dates
- 1 ½ tbsp. cacao powder
- ½ pitted avocado
- 2 peeled bananas
- 1 ½ ounces swiss chard

Here's how to do it:

1. Mix everything in a blender.
2. Puree ingredients until smooth in texture or you reach your desired consistency.

Chapter 2: Detoxification

Morning Magic Smoothie

Ingredients:

- Ice
- 1 tbsp. flax meal
- 1 scoop protein powder, flavor of choice
- 1/3 C. plain yogurt
- 1 frozen banana
- 1 C. cold coffee

Here's how to do it:

1. Mix everything in a blender.
2. Puree ingredients until smooth in texture or you reach your desired consistency.

Healthy Detox Smoothie

Ingredients:

- ½ C. coconut water
- ¼ cucumber
- ¼ C. blueberries
- 1 tbsp. fresh ginger
- 2-3 tbsp. lemon juice
- 1 C. spinach
- ½ frozen banana

Here's how to do it:

1. Mix everything in a blender.
2. Puree ingredients until smooth in texture or you reach your desired consistency.

Anti-Bloat Smoothie

Ingredients:

- Ice
- 1 tsp. apple cider vinegar
- 1-2 tbsp. fresh ginger
- ½ cucumber
- 1 frozen banana
- ½ C. coconut water

Here's how to do it:

1. Mix everything in a blender.
2. Puree ingredients until smooth in texture or you reach your desired consistency.

Green Detox Smoothie

Ingredients:

- 1 C. cold water
- 1 C. unsweetened almond milk
- ½ - 1 tsp. spirulina powder
- 2 tbsp. chia seeds
- 1 C. frozen pineapple
- 1 frozen ripe banana
- 1 peeled lemon
- 2 chopped celery stalks
- ½ chopped cucumber
- 1 ½ C. kale

Here's how to do it:

1. Mix everything in a blender.
2. Puree ingredients until smooth in texture or you reach your desired consistency.

Sunrise Detox Smoothie

Ingredients:

- 1 C. coconut water
- ½ C. frozen raspberries
- ½ C. pineapple
- ½ C. frozen mango
- 1 frozen banana
- Juice of 1 lemon

Here's how to do it:

1. Blend raspberries and set to the side.
2. 2Blend remaining ingredients until smooth.
3. Pour raspberry mixture into serving glass first, followed by mango mixture.

5-Ingredient Detox Smoothie

Ingredients:

- 1 C. fruit juice of choice (orange, pomegranate, etc.)
- 1 tbsp. flax seed meal
- ½ C. frozen banana
- 1 C. kale or spinach
- 1 C. frozen berries of choice

Here's how to do it:

1. Mix everything in a blender.
2. Puree ingredients until smooth in texture or you reach your desired consistency.

Golden Detox Smoothie

Ingredients:

Ice cubes
- ½ C. water
- ½ C. orange juice, freshly squeezed
- ½ C. fresh pineapple
- 1 peeled/diced carrot
- 2 tbsp. honey Greek yogurt
- 1 banana

Here's how to do it:

1. Mix everything in a blender.
2. Puree ingredients until smooth in texture or you reach your desired consistency.

Kale Recharge Smoothie

Ingredients:

- 4 ice cubes
- 1 C. water
- 1 tsp. lime juice
- 1 tbsp. parsley
- 1 tsp. grated ginger
- ½ C. chopped carrots
- ¾ C. kale
- ¾ C. spinach
- 1 frozen ripe banana

Here's how to do it:

1. Mix everything in a blender.
2. Puree ingredients until smooth in texture or you reach your desired consistency.

Toxic Blast Cleansing Smoothie

Ingredients:

- ½ C. water
- 2-3 ice cubes
- ½ C. strawberries, cored
- 1 banana
- 1 C. blueberries
- 1 handful spinach

Here's how to do it:

1. Mix everything in a blender.
2. Puree ingredients until smooth in texture or you reach your desired consistency.

Apple and Kale Green Detox Smoothie

Ingredients:

- 1 tsp. honey
- 1 tbsp. ground flax seed
- ½ green or red apple, cored/chopped
- 1 chopped celery stalk
- 1 ½ C. chopped kale
- ¾ C. ice
- 2/3 C. unsweetened almond milk

Here's how to do it:

1. Mix everything in a blender.
2. Puree ingredients until smooth in texture or you reach your desired consistency.

Sweet Spirit Smoothie

Ingredients:

- 1 scoop vanilla protein powder
- 1 tsp. spirulina
- ½ C. almond milk
- ¼ avocado
- ½ C. blueberries
- ½ banana

Here's how to do it:

1. Mix everything in a blender.
2. Puree ingredients until smooth in texture or you reach your desired consistency.

Alkalinity Bliss Smoothie .

Ingredients:

- 1 scoop protein powder, your choice of flavor
- 1 tsp. chia seeds
- 1 C. almond milk
- ¼ C. coconut water
- 1 packed cup of spinach
- ¼ avocado
- ½ pear

Here's how to do it:

1. Mix everything in a blender.
2. Puree ingredients until smooth in texture or you reach your desired consistency.

Strawberry Fields Smoothie

Ingredients:

- 1 ½ C. spinach
- 1 banana
- 1 peeled orange
- 1 tbsp. lemon zest
- 2 C. strawberries
- 3 C. cashew milk

Here's how to do it:

1. Mix everything in a blender.
2. Puree ingredients until smooth in texture or you reach your desired consistency.

Sicilian Smoothie

Ingredients:

- 1 seeded red jalapeno pepper
- 1 C. spinach
- 1 C. watercress
- 4 celery stalks
- 4 garlic cloves
- 2 red bell peppers
- 3 tomatoes
- 6 carrots

Here's how to do it:

1. Mix everything in a blender.
2. Puree ingredients until smooth in texture or you reach your desired consistency.

Lemon Blueberry Smoothie

Ingredients:

- 1 lemon
- ¼ C. blueberries
- 1 C. alkaline water

Here's how to do it:

1. Mix everything in a blender.
2. Puree ingredients until smooth in texture or you reach your desired consistency.

Chapter 4: Weight Loss

Blueberry Smoothie

Ingredients:

- 1 tbsp. flax seed oil
- 1 banana
- 1 C. blueberries

Here's how to do it:

1. Mix everything in a blender.
2. Puree ingredients until smooth in texture or you reach your desired consistency.

Chocolate Raspberry Smoothie

Ingredients:

- ½ C. unsweetened almond milk
- ¼ C. chocolate chips
- 1 C. raspberries

Here's how to do it:

1. Mix everything in a blender.
2. Puree ingredients until smooth in texture or you reach your desired consistency.

Silky Mango Smoothie

Ingredients:

- 2 C. mango
- ½ C. avocado
- 1 C. fresh orange juice

- ¼ C. lime juice

Here's how to do it:

1. Mix everything in a blender.
2. Puree ingredients until smooth in texture or you reach your desired consistency.

Green Almond Smoothie

Ingredients:

- ½ C. unsweetened almond milk
- ¼ C. natural almond butter
- 1 banana
- 1 ½ C. kale

Here's how to do it:

1. Mix everything in a blender.
2. Puree ingredients until smooth in texture or you reach your desired consistency.

Lemon Orange Citrus Smoothie

Ingredients:

- ½ C. skim milk
- ¼ C. lemon yogurt
- 1 peeled orange
- 2 tbsp. flax seed oil
- 3-4 ice cubes

Here's how to do it:

1. Mix everything in a blender.
2. Puree ingredients until smooth in texture or you reach your desired consistency.

Apple Blaster Smoothie

Ingredients:

- ½ C. water
- 2 celery stalks
- 1-inch piece ginger, grated
- 3 carrots
- 2 apples of choice

Here's how to do it:

1. Mix everything in a blender.
2. Puree ingredients until smooth in texture or you reach your desired consistency.

All-Rounder Smoothie

Ingredients:

- 1 thumb of grated ginger
- Handful of spinach
- 1 C. water
- 1 lemon

Here's how to do it:

1. Mix everything in a blender.
2. Puree ingredients until smooth in texture or you reach your desired consistency.

Fat Burning Green Smoothie

Ingredients:

- 1 tbsp. chia seeds
- ½ tsp. ginger
- 1 C. frozen pineapple chunks

- 1 C. unsweetened almond milk
- 1 banana
- 2 handfuls baby spinach

Here's how to do it:

1. Mix everything in a blender.
2. Puree ingredients until smooth in texture or you reach your desired consistency.

Mango Passion Fruit Smoothie

Ingredients:

- 1 ½ C. orange juice
- 1 mango
- 1 banana
- 3 passion fruits

Here's how to do it:

1. Mix everything in a blender.
2. Puree ingredients until smooth in texture or you reach your desired consistency.

Fruity Green Smoothie

Ingredients:

- 1 tsp. lemon juice
- 1 tsp. grated ginger
- 1 ½ C. water
- 1 chopped pear
- 2 C. spinach

Here's how to do it:

1. Mix everything in a blender.

2. Puree ingredients until smooth in texture or you reach your desired consistency.

Kale Chia Seed Smoothie

Ingredients:

- 1 tsp. lemon juice
- 1 C. plain yogurt
- 1 tbsp. chia seeds
- 1 banana
- 2 kale leaves

Here's how to do it:

1. Mix everything in a blender.
2. Puree ingredients until smooth in texture or you reach your desired consistency.

Zesty Fat Burner Smoothie

Ingredients:

- 1 tbsp. flax seeds
- 1 C. water
- 1 lemon
- 3 slices of pineapple

Here's how to do it:

1. Mix everything in a blender.
2. Puree ingredients until smooth in texture or you reach your desired consistency.

Matcha Pear Green Protein Smoothie

Ingredients:

- ½ tsp. matcha tea powder
- 1 pear
- 1 C. spinach
- 1 C. unsweetened almond milk
- 2 scoops vanilla protein powder

Here's how to do it:

1. Mix everything in a blender.
2. Puree ingredients until smooth in texture or you reach your desired consistency.

Watermelon Smoothie

Ingredients:

- 12 ice cubes
- 1 C. lemon sherbet
- 6 C. seedless watermelon

Here's how to do it:

1. Mix everything in a blender.
2. Puree ingredients until smooth in texture or you reach your desired consistency.

Spinach Avocado Smoothie

Ingredients:

- 1 C. water
- 1 tbsp. peanut butter
- 1 banana

- 1 C. spinach
- 1 avocado

Here's how to do it:

1. Mix everything in a blender.
2. Puree ingredients until smooth in texture or you reach your desired consistency.

Chapter 5: Radiant Skin

Powerhouse Pumpkin Smoothie

Ingredients:

- ½ tsp. pumpkin pie spice
- 2 tbsp. ground flaxseed
- ¼ avocado
- ½ C. water
- 7 ounces 2% Greek yogurt
- ½ C. canned pure pumpkin

Here's how to do it:

1. Mix everything in a blender.
2. Puree ingredients until smooth in texture or you reach your desired consistency.

Mango Surprise Smoothie

Ingredients:

- 6 ice cubes
- 1 tbsp. sugar
- 1 tbsp. lime juice
- ¼ C. fat-free vanilla yogurt
- ¼ C. mashed avocado
- ¼ C. mango cubes
- ½ C. mango juice

Here's how to do it:

1. Mix everything in a blender.
2. Puree ingredients until smooth in texture or you reach your desired consistency.

Super Green Smoothie

Ingredients:

- ¼ C. chopped mint
- ¼ C. chopped parsley
- 1 C. chilled orange juice
- 2 chopped celery ribs
- 1 ¼ C. frozen cubed mango
- 1 ¼ C. chopped kale

Here's how to do it:

1. Mix everything in a blender.
2. Puree ingredients until smooth in texture or you reach your desired consistency.

Gingered Cantaloupe Smoothie

Ingredients:

- ½ tsp. grated ginger
- 3 tbsp. sugar
- 6 ounces low-fat plain yogurt
- 2 C. cubed cantaloupe
- 20 ice cubes

Here's how to do it:

1. Mix everything in a blender.
2. Puree ingredients until smooth in texture or you reach your desired consistency.

Healthy High C Smoothie

Ingredients:

- ¼ C. ice cubes
- 1 chopped celery rib
- ½ C. cilantro sprigs
- ½ C. orange or tangerine juice
- 2 peeled/chopped kiwis
- 1 C. chopped kale

Here's how to do it:

1. Mix everything in a blender.
2. Puree ingredients until smooth in texture or you reach your desired consistency.

Carrot Cake Smoothie

Ingredients:

- Ice cubes
- 2g glucomannan
- ¼ tsp. cinnamon
- 1 tsp. flaxseed oil
- 1 tbsp. softened cream cheese
- 2 tbsp. toasted wheat germ
- 1 scoop vanilla protein powder
- ½ C. unsweetened carrot juice

Here's how to do it:

1. Mix everything in a blender.
2. Puree ingredients until smooth in texture or you reach your desired consistency.

Winter Greens Smoothie

Ingredients:

- 1 cored/chopped apple
- 1 frozen/peeled/sliced banana
- 4 sliced/frozen broccoli florets
- 1 C. chopped kale
- 1 C. spinach
- ½ C. orange juice
- ¼ C. carrot juice

Here's how to do it:

1. Mix everything in a blender.
2. Puree ingredients until smooth in texture or you reach your desired consistency.

Apricot Smoothie

Ingredients:

- 1/8 tsp. almond extract
- 2/3 C. non-fat vanilla frozen yogurt
- 1 C. skim milk
- 12 pitted apricot halves

Here's how to do it:

1. Mix everything in a blender.
2. Puree ingredients until smooth in texture or you reach your desired consistency.

Veggie and Fruit Smoothie

Ingredients:

- 6 baby carrots
- ½ sliced banana
- 1 C. spinach
- 1 C. frozen berries
- ½ C. low-fat vanilla yogurt
- ½ C. orange juice

Here's how to do it:

1. Mix everything in a blender.
2. Puree ingredients until smooth in texture or you reach your desired consistency.

Green Goddess Smoothie

Ingredients:

- ¼ C. mint leaves
- ½ C. orange juice
- ½ C. frozen vanilla yogurt
- 1 peeled/chopped kiwi
- ½ peeled avocado
- 1 C. cucumber chunks
- 1 C. baby spinach

Here's how to do it:

1. Mix everything in a blender.
2. Puree ingredients until smooth in texture or you reach your desired consistency.

Cinnamon Apple Crumble Smoothie

Ingredients:

- 1 C. ice
- 1 C. water
- ¼ C. walnuts
- 1 tbsp. quinoa flakes
- 1 tsp. cinnamon
- 2 chopped apples
- 1 ½ ounces swiss chard

Here's how to do it:

1. Mix everything in a blender.
2. Puree ingredients until smooth in texture or you reach your desired consistency.

Celery Apple Refresher Smoothie

Ingredients:

- 1 C. ice
- 1 C. water
- ½ tsp. moringa
- 2 tbsp. raw hazelnuts
- 3 sprigs of mint
- 1 chopped apple
- 2 celery ribs
- 1 ½ ounce collard greens

Here's how to do it:

1. Mix everything in a blender.
2. Puree ingredients until smooth in texture or you reach your desired consistency.

Summer Strawberry Sunset Smoothie

Ingredients:

- 1 C. ice
- 1 C. vanilla almond milk
- 1 tbsp. coconut flakes
- 1 peeled blood orange
- 1 chopped pear
- 1 C. strawberries

Here's how to do it:

1. Mix everything in a blender.
2. Puree ingredients until smooth in texture or you reach your desired consistency.

Ginger Plum Flower Smoothie

Ingredients:

- 1 C. ice
- 1 C. water
- 1 tbsp. chia seeds
- ½ juiced lemon
- ½ an inch of peeled ginger
- 2 pitted plums
- 1 peeled orange
- 4 ounces chopped beets

Here's how to do it:

1. Mix everything in a blender.
2. Puree ingredients until smooth in texture or you reach your desired consistency.

Yellow Turmeric Ginger Smoothie

Ingredients:

- 1 C. ice
- 1 C. water
- 1 tbsp. hemp seed
- ½ an inch peeled ginger
- ½ tsp. turmeric
- 1-ounce of kumquats
- 1 peeled orange
- 1 chopped yellow squash

Here's how to do it:

1. Mix everything in a blender.
2. Puree ingredients until smooth in texture or you reach your desired consistency.

Chapter 6: Energy Boost

Mango, Mandarin, Cayenne Smoothie

Ingredients:

- 1 tsp. vanilla
- 1/8 tsp. cayenne powder
- 1 tbsp. honey
- 1 C. mango chunks
- 1 peeled/seeded mandarin orange
- 1 C. unsweetened almond milk

Here's how to do it:

1. Mix everything in a blender.
2. Puree ingredients until smooth in texture or you reach your desired consistency.

Key Lime Pie Smoothie

Ingredients:

- 2 tbsp. honey
- 1 tsp. vanilla
- 2 bananas
- 1 avocado
- ½ C. lime juice
- 1 ½ C. apple juice

Here's how to do it:

1. Mix everything in a blender.
2. Puree ingredients until smooth in texture or you reach your desired consistency.

Banana, Mint, Coconut Water Smoothie

Ingredients:

- 1 tsp. vanilla
- 1 tbsp. hemp seeds
- 2 C. coconut water
- 1 handful mint leaves
- 5 frozen bananas

Here's how to do it:

1. Mix everything in a blender.
2. Puree ingredients until smooth in texture or you reach your desired consistency.

Raspberry, Cacao, Maca Smoothie

Ingredients:

- ½ tsp. cinnamon
- 1 tsp. lucuma powder
- 1 tsp. vanilla
- 1 tsp. maca powder
- ¼ C. cashews
- 1 tbsp. raw cacao nibs
- 1 C. baby spinach
- ½ C. frozen raspberries

Here's how to do it:

1. Mix everything in a blender.
2. Puree ingredients until smooth in texture or you reach your desired consistency.

Ginger, Pear, Lemongrass Smoothie

Ingredients:

- 2 C. coconut milk
- 1 tsp. raw honey
- ¼ inch ginger root
- 1-2 stalks lemongrass
- 1 frozen banana
- 1 cored pear

Here's how to do it:

1. Mix everything in a blender.
2. Puree ingredients until smooth in texture or you reach your desired consistency.

Banana, Turmeric, Chai Smoothie

Ingredients:

- ¼ inch turmeric root
- ¼ inch ginger root
- 1 tsp. vanilla
- 1 tsp. lucuma powder
- 1-2 tsp. raw honey
- ¼ C. rolled oats
- 2 C. chilled chai tea
- 2 frozen bananas

Here's how to do it:

1. Mix everything in a blender.
2. Puree ingredients until smooth in texture or you reach your desired consistency.

Forest Berry and Brazil Nut Smoothie

Ingredients:

- 2 C. apple juice
- 1 tsp. guarana powder
- ¼ C. Brazil nuts
- 1 C. baby spinach
- 1 frozen banana
- 2 C. frozen mixed berries
- Raw honey, to taste

Here's how to do it:

1. Mix everything in a blender.
2. Puree ingredients until smooth in texture or you reach your desired consistency.
3. Adjust sweetness of smoothie with raw honey.

Chocolate, Chia, Banana Smoothie

Ingredients:

- 1 tsp. lucuma powder
- 1 tsp. vanilla
- 2 C. walnut milk
- 1 tbsp. raw cacao nibs
- 2 tbsp. soaked chia seeds
- 1 C. baby spinach
- 2 frozen bananas

Here's how to do it:

1. Mix everything in a blender.
2. Puree ingredients until smooth in texture or you reach your desired consistency.

Banana Matcha Energizing Smoothie

Ingredients:

- 1-2 tsp. honey
- 1-2 tsp. matcha powder
- 2 C. almond milk
- 1 C. romaine lettuce
- 2 frozen bananas

Here's how to do it:

1. Mix everything in a blender.
2. Puree ingredients until smooth in texture or you reach your desired consistency.

Kale and Lavender Energizing Smoothie

Ingredients:

- 1 tsp. vanilla
- 1 tsp. lucuma powder
- ¼ C. raw cashews
- ½ C. rolled oats
- 1 C. apple juice
- 1 C. kale
- 1 C. mulberries
- 1 frozen banana

Here's how to do it:

1. Mix everything in a blender.
2. Puree ingredients until smooth in texture or you reach your desired consistency.

Peach Vanilla Yogurt Smoothie

Ingredients:

- ½ C. non-fat vanilla frozen yogurt
- 1 peach
- 1 C. soy milk

Here's how to do it:

1. Mix everything in a blender.
2. Puree ingredients until smooth in texture or you reach your desired consistency.

Berry Vanilla Banana Smoothie

Ingredients:

- ¼ tsp. vanilla
- ½ frozen banana
- ¼ C. frozen red grapes
- ¼ C. frozen blackberries
- ¼ C. frozen blueberries
- 1/3 C. 1%-fat cottage cheese
- 1 C. non-fat milk

Here's how to do it:

1. Mix everything in a blender.
2. Puree ingredients until smooth in texture or you reach your desired consistency.

Green Grape Smoothie

Ingredients:

- 2 C. ice
- ½ C. water
- 1 tsp. chia seeds
- 1 banana
- 1 peeled orange
- 1 cored pear
- 1 C. green grapes
- 1 C. chopped kale
- 1 C. spinach

Here's how to do it:

1. Mix everything in a blender.
2. Puree ingredients until smooth in texture or you reach your desired consistency.

Peach and Orange Smoothie

Ingredients:

- 1 C. fat-free milk
- 2 tbsp. flaxseed
- ½ C. orange juice
- 2 C. sliced peaches
- 2 C. light ice cream

Here's how to do it:

1. Mix everything in a blender.
2. Puree ingredients until smooth in texture or you reach your desired consistency.

Mango Strawberry Smoothie

Ingredients:

- 1 tsp. chia seeds
- ¼ C. green tea
- 1 tbsp. Greek yogurt
- ¼ C. red bell pepper
- ¼ C. chopped carrot
- ¼ C. kale
- ¼ C. frozen peach slices
- ¼ C. red grapes
- ½ C. frozen mango
- 1 C. strawberries

Here's how to do it:

1. Mix everything in a blender.
2. Puree ingredients until smooth in texture or you reach your desired consistency.

Chapter 7: Anti-Aging

Blueberry Breeze Smoothie

Ingredients:

- 1 handful mint
- 1 tsp. chia seeds
- 1 tbsp. lemon juice
- 1 C. coconut water
- 1 C. strawberries
- 1 C. frozen blueberries

Here's how to do it:
1. Mix everything in a blender.
2. Puree ingredients until smooth in texture or you reach your desired consistency.

Tropical Chia Smoothie

Ingredients:

- 1 C. coconut water
- 1 tbsp. chia seeds
- 1 C. pineapple
- ½ C. mango

Here's how to do it:

1. Mix everything in a blender.
2. Puree ingredients until smooth in texture or you reach your desired consistency.

Cacao Banana Dream Smoothie

Ingredients:

- 1 C. unsweetened almond milk
- 1 tbsp. cacao powder
- 6 strawberries
- 1 banana

Here's how to do it:

1. Mix everything in a blender.
2. Puree ingredients until smooth in texture or you reach your desired consistency.

Berry Power Smoothie

Ingredients:

- Ice cubes
- ½ C. unsweetened orange juice
- 1 tbsp. honey
- 1 handfuls sesame seeds
- ½ C. blueberries
- ½ C. frozen strawberries

Here's how to do it:

1. Mix everything in a blender.
2. Puree ingredients until smooth in texture or you reach your desired consistency.

Tart Green Monster Smoothie

Here's how to do it:

- Few ice cubes
- 1 tbsp. chia seeds
- 1 apple
- 1 handful kale
- 1 banana
- ½ - 1 C. unsweetened almond milk

Here's how to do it:

1. Mix everything in a blender.
2. Puree ingredients until smooth in texture or you reach your desired consistency.

Tropical Delight Smoothie

Ingredients:

- 2-3 ice cubes
- 1 C. orange juice
- 1 handful flaxseeds
- 2 kiwis
- 2 mangoes
- Half a pineapple

Here's how to do it:

1. Mix everything in a blender.
2. Puree ingredients until smooth in texture or you reach your desired consistency.

Cacao and Date Delight Smoothie

Ingredients:

- Pinch of cinnamon
- ½ C. unsweetened almond milk
- ¼ tsp. vanilla
- 1 tbsp. cacao powder
- 4 walnuts halves
- 5 pitted dates

Here's how to do it:

1. Mix everything in a blender.
2. Puree ingredients until smooth in texture or you reach your desired consistency.

Anti-Aging Mixed Berry Smoothie

Ingredients:

- 4 ice cubes
- ½ banana
- 1 tbsp. honey
- 1 tbsp. flaxseeds
- ½ C. almond milk
- ½ C. raspberries
- 1 C. blueberries

Here's how to do it:

1. Mix everything in a blender.
2. Puree ingredients until smooth in texture or you reach your desired consistency.

Blueberry Peach Smoothie

Ingredients:

- ¾ C. unsweetened vanilla almond milk
- 1 ½ C. sliced peaches
- ½ C. frozen blueberries

Here's how to do it:

1. Mix everything in a blender.
2. Puree ingredients until smooth in texture or you reach your desired consistency.

Berry Beauty Smoothie

Ingredients:

- ¼ C. water
- ¾ C. soy milk
- 1 tbsp. flaxseed
- ½ C. chopped pineapple
- ½ C. frozen mixed berries
- ¼ C. peeled/sliced kiwi
- 1 banana

Here's how to do it:

1. Mix everything in a blender.
2. Puree ingredients until smooth in texture or you reach your desired consistency.

Vitamin E Green Smoothie

Ingredients:

- 1 C. spinach
- ½ avocado
- ¼ C. lemon juice
- 1 C. almond milk
- ¼ C. sunflower seeds
- 1 banana

Here's how to do it:

1. Mix everything in a blender.
2. Puree ingredients until smooth in texture or you reach your desired consistency.

Tropically Aging Smoothie

Ingredients:

- 1 C. blueberries
- ¼ C. lemon juice
- 1 C. coconut water
- 1 C. strawberries
- Handful mint
- ¼ C. chia seeds

Here's how to do it:

1. Mix everything in a blender.
2. Puree ingredients until smooth in texture or you reach your desired consistency.

Leafy Anti-Aging Power Smoothie

Ingredients:

- 2 C. kale leaves
- ¼ C. lemon juice
- 2 cored apples
- 1 C. chopped carrot
- 1 C. coconut water

Here's how to do it:

1. Mix everything in a blender.
2. Puree ingredients until smooth in texture or you reach your desired consistency.

Chia Smoothie

Ingredients:

- 1 C. coconut water
- 2 C. mango
- 1 C. pineapple
- ¼ C. chia seeds

Here's how to do it:

1. Mix everything in a blender.
2. Puree ingredients until smooth in texture or you reach your desired consistency.

Cherry Shake Smoothie

Ingredients:

- ½ banana
- 2-3 C. spinach
- 1 C. cherries
- 2 tbsp. flax oil
- 1 C. coconut milk

Here's how to do it:

1. Mix everything in a blender.
2. Puree ingredients until smooth in texture or you reach your desired consistency.

Chapter 8: Superfoods

Strawberry Goji Berry Smoothie

Ingredients:

- Ice
- 2 C. almond milk
- 2 tsp. honey
- 1 C. strawberries
- 2 tbsp. dried goji berries

Here's how to do it:

1. Mix everything in a blender.
2. Puree ingredients until smooth in texture or you reach your desired consistency.

Kick Booty Kale Smoothie

Ingredients:

- 1-3 tsp. honey
- 2 tbsp. peanut butter
- ¼ c. frozen pineapple
- ¼ C. Greek yogurt
- 1 frozen banana
- ¾ C. almond milk
- 2 C. kale

Here's how to do it:

1. Mix everything in a blender.
2. Puree ingredients until smooth in texture or you reach your desired consistency.

Blueberry Flax Smoothie

Ingredients:

- 1 C. coconut milk
- ¼ C. Greek yogurt
- Handful of spinach
- 1 tbsp. flaxseed
- 1 C. frozen blueberries

Here's how to do it:

1. Mix everything in a blender.
2. Puree ingredients until smooth in texture or you reach your desired consistency.

Spiced Green Tea Smoothie

Ingredients:

- 6-8 ice cubes
- 2 tbsp. plain yogurt
- 1 pear
- 2 tsp. honey
- Juice of 1 lemon
- 1/8 tsp. cayenne pepper
- ¾ C. chilled green tea

Here's how to do it:

1. Mix everything in a blender.
2. Puree ingredients until smooth in texture or you reach your desired consistency.

Antioxidant Berry Smoothie Bowl

Ingredients:

- ¼ C. pomegranate seeds
- 1 tbsp. coconut flakes
- 1 tbsp. pepitas
- 1 tsp. chia seeds
- Fresh blackberries and raspberries
- ½ banana
- ½ C. almond milk
- 1 tbsp. hemp seeds
- ½ C. frozen berries
- 1 frozen banana

Here's how to do it:

1. Mix everything in a blender.
2. Puree ingredients until smooth in texture or you reach your desired consistency.
3. Pour smoothie mixture into bowl and top with desired toppings.

Chocolate Avocado Smoothie

Ingredients:

- 2 C. coconut milk
- 1-2 tbsp. cocoa powder
- ½ C. frozen raspberries
- 2 frozen bananas
- 1 avocado

Here's how to do it:

1. Mix everything in a blender.
2. Puree ingredients until smooth in texture or you reach your desired consistency.

Plum Quinoa Smoothie

Ingredients:

- 4-5 ice cubes
- ¼ tsp. cinnamon
- 1 tsp. vanilla
- 1 C. almond milk
- ¼ C. cooked quinoa
- ½ frozen banana
- 1 pitted/chopped ripe plum

Here's how to do it:

1. Mix everything in a blender.
2. Puree ingredients until smooth in texture or you reach your desired consistency.

Oat Coconut Smoothie

Ingredients:

- ½ C. ice
- 1/3 C. orange juice
- 1 tbsp. honey
- 2 tbsp. coconut oil
- 1/3 C. Greek yogurt
- ¼ C. rolled oats

- ½ banana

Here's how to do it:

Mix everything in a blender.
1. Puree ingredients until smooth in texture or you reach your desired consistency.

Swamp Smoothie

Ingredients:

- 1 tbsp. hemp seeds
- 3 tbsp. hemp protein powder
- 1 tbsp. cacao powder
- 1 C. almond milk
- 1 handful spinach
- ½ C. chopped broccoli
- ½ banana
- 1 C. strawberries

Here's how to do it:

2. Mix everything in a blender.
3. Puree ingredients until smooth in texture or you reach your desired consistency.

Coconut Turmeric Smoothie

Ingredients:

- 1 tsp. maca
- 1 tsp. chia seeds
- ½ tsp. ginger
- ½ tsp. cinnamon
- ½ - 1 tsp. turmeric
- 1 tbsp. coconut oil
- 1 frozen banana
- ½ C. frozen pineapple
- 1 C. coconut milk

Here's how to do it:

1. Mix everything in a blender.
2. Puree ingredients until smooth in texture or you reach your desired consistency.

Green Apple Smoothie

Ingredients:

- 1 tbsp. chia seeds
- ½ tsp. cinnamon
- 1 tsp. minced ginger
- 1 banana
- 1 C. orange juice
- 1 apple
- 1 ½ C. kale

Here's how to do it:

1. Mix everything in a blender.

2. Puree ingredients until smooth in texture or you reach your desired consistency.

Babe Ruth Smoothie

Ingredients:

- 1 tbsp. chia seeds
- 1 C. spinach
- ½ C. Greek yogurt
- 2 C. orange juice
- 1 banana
- ½ C. pineapple
- 1 C. strawberries

Here's how to do it:

1. Mix everything in a blender.
2. Puree ingredients until smooth in texture or you reach your desired consistency.

Sweet Cherry Almond Smoothie

Ingredients:

- Ice
- 1 banana
- 1 scoop protein powder
- 1 C. almond milk
- 1 ½ C. frozen cherries

Here's how to do it:

1. Mix everything in a blender.
2. Puree ingredients until smooth in texture or you reach your desired consistency.

Lovely Greens Smoothie

Ingredients:

- 1 banana
- Ice
- 1 ½ C. orange juice
- ½ C. grapes
- 2 C. spinach
- 1 C. pineapple

Here's how to do it:

1. Mix everything in a blender.
2. Puree ingredients until smooth in texture or you reach your desired consistency.

Chocolate Powerhouse Smoothie

Ingredients:

- 1 tbsp. almond butter
- 1 banana
- 1 C. spinach
- ½ C. blueberries
- 1 scoop chocolate protein powder
- 1 C. coconut milk
- Ice

Here's how to do it:

1. Mix everything in a blender.
2. Puree ingredients until smooth in texture or you reach your desired consistency.

Conclusion

I want to congratulate you for making it to the end of The Complete Healthy Smoothie Recipe Book.

If you are serious about getting your health back on track and becoming the healthiest version of yourself possible, then all of these smoothie recipes will come in handy any time of day when you are crunched for time!

Stop falling victim to fat and carb-filled convenience foods and whip up a smoothie instead! As you have read, all of the smoothie recipes have something a bit different to offer your body than the next. I hope that you find a smoothie recipe for all parts of your day to help you feel better, energized, and motivated to take on life each day!

The Complete Soup Maker Recipe Book

Introduction

When it comes to taking care of our health, it can be overwhelming with the hundreds of thousands of recipes out there; which ones are the best for us? Which ones take little time to make? Which ones have the best and easily located ingredients?

Thankfully, you are just one cookbook away from being able to whip up a variety of soups in a plethora of machines in your very own kitchen! You can be the master of time with your slow cooker, instant pot, or good old-fashioned stove. No matter the time, energy, or ingredients you have, this book has a soup recipe suited for your needs in the here and now.

This specifically soup cookbook is packed with a variety of soups from hearty and meaty to chilled and oh so simple to make. Whether you are looking to make the most of your time as you make meals, lose weight, or just physically feel better, all of these soups will help you do just that!

While there is a plethora of soup-related recipe cookbooks on the market today, there is none quite like this one, which is why I want to thank you again for choosing this one. Every effort was made to ensure it is full of as much useful information as possible, please enjoy!

Chapter 1: Vegetable Soups

Loaded Cauliflower Soup

What's in it:

- ½ C. half & half
- 1 C. shredded sharp cheddar cheese
- 3 C. chicken stock
- 1 tsp. salt
- 1 head cauliflower
- 2 tbsp. Butter
- ½ chopped onion
- 4 ounces cream cheese
- 1 tsp. garlic powder

Toppings:

- Green onions
- 8-10 strips bacon
- Sour cream
- Grated sharp cheddar cheese

How it's made:

1. Peel your onion and chop into pieces.
2. Cut off leaves of cauliflower and chop into pieces.
3. Press SAUTE on instant pot. Melt butter and pour in onion, sautéing 2-3 minutes.
4. Add cauliflower, salt, garlic powder, and chicken stock.
5. Lock lid and press MANUAL. Cook on HIGH 5 minutes.
6. Perform quick release.
7. As soup cooks, cook bacon.
8. Check to see if cauliflower is tender. Then push KEEP WARM on pot.

9. With an immersion blender, puree soup. Add more stock to adjust thickness if you choose.
10. Pour in cream cheese and grated cheese, stirring to combine.
11. Then add half & half, and season with pepper and salt to achieve desired taste.
12. Serve soup hot along with green onion, crumbled bacon, sour cream, and grated cheese.

Unstuffed Pepper Soup

What's in it:

- 2 C./500ml water
- 1-pound ground beef
- 2 tsp./10ml Italian seasoning
- 2 tbsp./30ml coconut aminos
- 2 10-ounce cans Rotel
- 8-ounce can tomato sauce – no sugar added
- 2 crushed garlic cloves
- 1 C./250 ml diced onion
- 1 piece of each pepper:
  - Yellow
  - Red
  - Green
  - Orange

How it's made:

1. Mix together all recipe components.
2. Pour mixture into crockpot.
3. Set to cook on low 6-8 hours.

Broccoli Cheese Soup

What's in it:

- 1 tsp. pepper and salt
- 1 C. carrots – shredded
- ¼ tsp. garlic powder
- 1 bunch broccoli
- 1 C. heavy cream
- 4 C. chicken stock
- 1 tbsp. onion powder
- 2 C. shredded cheddar cheese

How it's made:

1. Turn instant pot to SAUTE.
2. Place butter in a pot and melt.
3. Pour in pepper, salt, onion powder, garlic powder, chicken stock, carrots and broccoli into the instant pot. Set to cook on HIGH for 5 minutes.
4. Perform quick release.
5. Mix in heavy cream and cheddar cheese.

Butternut Squash Soup

What's in it:

- ½ C. unsweetened coconut milk
- Pinch of nutmeg
- Pinch of cinnamon
- A dash of pepper
- 1 diced onion
- 1 sprig sage
- 1 butternut squash
- 1 granny smith apple

- A dash of cayenne pepper
- 1 carrot
- 2 cloves minced/peeled garlic
- 2 C. vegetable stock
- ½ tsp. salt

How it's made:

1. Cut up squash, carrots, and apple.
2. Pour vegetable stock into cooker along with nutmeg, cinnamon, cayenne, pepper, salt, onion, sage, butternut squash, apple, carrot, and garlic.
3. Set to heat on low 6-8 hours or set to heat 3 to 4 hours on high. Squash should be tender.
4. Remove sage and stir in coconut milk.
5. With an immersion blender, puree soup until its smooth. Season with cayenne, pepper, and salt if needed to achieve desired taste.

Autumn Beef and Veggie Stew

What's in it:

- 1 tsp. turmeric powder
- 4-5 zucchinis
- 1 rutabaga
- 1 ½ tsp. salt
- 2 cinnamon sticks
- 1 tsp. coriander seeds
- 1 tsp. ginger
- 1 tbsp. paprika
- 2 tbsp. cumin
- 1 C. vegetable stock
- 14-ounce can chopped tomatoes
- 4 garlic cloves

- 1 tsp. chili powder
- 1 white onion
- ½ C. ghee
- 2 bay leaves
- 3 ½ pounds boneless braising steaks

How it's made:

1. Turn crockpot to high.
2. Pat down steaks and season with pepper and salt.
3. Place steaks into a skillet with ¼ cup of ghee. Sear until just browned lightly. Place into the crockpot.
4. Peel and dice garlic and onion. Put into a pan with ghee that remains, sautéing until fragrant.
5. Add turmeric, coriander, chili powder, ginger, cumin, broth, paprika, and tomatoes to pot. Then add bay leaves and cinnamon sticks.
6. Set to cook on high 3 hours.
7. Push meat to one side of the pot.
8. Peel and dice rutabaga and add to crockpot.
9. Add rutabaga to other side. Cook another 60 minutes
10. Dice zucchini. Add zucchini to the same side as rutabaga and mix well to combine with cooking juices.
11. Discard bay leaves and cinnamon sticks.
12. Cook another 2 hours. Once zucchini and rutabaga are tender to the touch of a fork, the stew is done!

Cabbage Stew

What's in it:

- 8-ounce can tomato sauce
- 8-ounce can whole plum tomatoes
- 5 sliced celery stalks
- 8 ounces shredded cabbage
- 2 bay leaves
- ¼ tsp./1.25ml Pepper
- 1 tsp./5ml Greek seasoning
- 2 chopped onion
- 1 1/3 C./75 ml hot chicken broth
- 1 beef boullion cube
- 2 pounds beef stew meat

How it's made:

1. In a pan, brown stew meat 5 minutes. Drain grease.
2. Stir boullion cube to broth until dissolved.
3. Add bay leaves, pepper, Greek seasoning, and onions to broth mixture.
4. Add stew meat and broth mixture to crockpot. Stir well to combine.
5. Set to cook on low 7 hours or set to cook 4.5 to 5 hours on high.
6. Stir in cabbage.
7. Trash bay leaves before serving stew

French Onion Soup

What's in it:

- 6 tbsp. parmesan cheese
- ½ C. shredded Emmental cheese
- 2 tbsp. brown sugar
- ¾ C. shredded Gruyere cheese
- 8 slices French bread
- 1 bay leaf
- 4 sprigs thyme
- 3 tbsp. butter
- 1/3 C. dry sherry
- 1 minced clove garlic
- 1 tbsp. Worcestershire sauce
- 64 ounces beef broth
- 3 sliced white onions

How it's made:

1. Heat onions with brown sugar and butter in a pan 20 minutes until caramelized.
2. Once gold, pour into your cooker and pour in remaining recipe components, minus the cheeses.
3. Set to heat on low 6-8 hours.
4. Take out and discard bay leaf. Spoon mixture into bowls. Top with bread slices and cheese.
5. Broil 2-3 minutes until cheese becomes melted and bread is crisp.

Potato Soup

What's in it:

- 1 tsp. salt
- 12 ounces evaporated milk
- 1/3 C. all-purpose flour
- 3 tbsp. bacon grease
- 1 diced onion
- ½ C. Greek yogurt
- 2 pounds Yukon potatoes
- 3-4 C. chicken stock
- 1 C. shredded cheddar cheese
- 6 slices heated/diced bacon
- ½ tsp. pepper

How it's made:

1. Place onion, potatoes, 3 cups of chicken stock, and bacon in your cooker. Combine well. Set to heat on low 6-8 hours or set to heat to cook 3 to 4 hours on low till potatoes become tender.
2. Once soup is ready to eat, melt butter and mix in flour, stirring 1 minute. Gradually pour in evaporated milk until mixture becomes smooth. Bring to a simmer and let it heat until very thickened.
3. Pour milk mixture into the cooker. Then mix in yogurt, cheese, pepper, and salt.
4. For a thicker soup, mash potatoes a bit. If you like a thinner soup, add 1-2 cups of warmed stock. Use pepper and salt to reach desired taste.
5. Serve with toppings of choice.

Root Vegetable Stew

What's in it:

- ½ tsp. salt
- 1 tsp. ginger
- 1 minced clove garlic
- ¼ C. coconut aminos
- ¼ C. apple cider vinegar
- 1 chopped sweet potato
- 1 chopped onion
- ½ pound chopped parsnips
- ½ pound chopped carrots
- 1 pound chopped beef

How it's made:

1. Pour all recipe components into a cooker and stir to thoroughly incorporate.
2. Set cooker to heat on high 3 hours. Enjoy!

Sweet Potato, Chicken, and Quinoa Soup

What's in it:

- 5 C. chicken broth
- 1 packet chili seasoning mix
- 1 tsp. minced garlic
- 14.25 ounce can petite diced tomatoes
- 15.25 ounce can black beans
- 2 pounds sweet potatoes
- 1 C. quinoa
- 1 ½ pounds boneless skinless chicken breasts

How it's made:

1. Grease slow cooker. Trim fat from chicken breasts and place into the cooker.
2. Rinse quinoa and add to cooker with chicken.
3. Discard skins from potatoes and cut them into chunks. Add potatoes to the cooker.
4. Drain black beans and then rinse them. Add to cooker along with the can of tomatoes.
5. Set cooker to cook on high 3 to 5 hours.
6. Shred chicken with forks and mix mixture well to incorporate all ingredients.
7. Season with pepper and salt if needed and garnish with parsley.

Snap Pea and Lettuce Soup

What's in it:

- ½ C. buttermilk
- 3 tbsp. tarragon
- 2 chopped romaine hearts
- 1-pound trimmed snap peas
- 2 peeled Yukon Gold potatoes
- 8 C. chicken stock
- ¼ C. butter
- 2 sliced leeks

How it's made:

1. Cook your leeks in butter till tender.
   Pour chicken stock and potatoes in and simmer till tender.
2. Add romaine hearts and snap peas, simmering till they are bright green.
3. Puree mixture in batches with tarragon till smooth in texture and then strain.
4. Mix in buttermilk and season with pepper and salt.

Chapter 2: Meaty Soups and Stews

Honey Balsamic Beef Stew

What's in it:

- 1 tbsp. Worcestershire sauce
- 2 tbsp. cornstarch
- ¼ tsp. pepper
- 1 tsp. seasoning salt
- 1/3 C. liquid honey
- 1/3 C. balsamic vinegar
- ¼ C. low-sodium beef broth
- 2 tbsp. tomato paste
- ½ chopped onion
- 2 peeled/chopped carrots
- 1 chopped stalk celery
- 1-pound stewing beef
- 2 tsp. minced garlic
- 1-pound little potatoes

How it's made:

1. Pour onions, carrots, celery, beef, and potatoes into a cooker.
2. Mix pepper, salt, cornstarch, garlic, Worcestershire sauce, tomato paste, honey, vinegar, and broth together. Pour into the cooker.
3. Set to heat on low 8 hours until carrots and potatoes become softened.

Chicken Bacon Chowder

What's in it:

- 1 tsp. thyme
- 1 tsp. salt
- 1 pound cooked and crumbled bacon
- 1 C. heavy cream
- 8 ounces cream cheese
- 1 pound chicken breasts
- 2 C. chicken stock
- 1 tsp. pepper
- 4 tbsp. butter
- 1 thinly sliced sweet onion
- 6 ounces sliced cremini mushrooms
- 2 diced celery ribs
- 1 trimmed and sliced leek
- 1 tsp. garlic powder
- 1 chopped shallot
- 4 minced garlic cloves

How it's made:

1. Turn crockpot to low. Add pepper, salt, 1 cup of stock, 2 tablespoons of butter, onions, mushrooms, leek, celery, shallot, and garlic. Cover and cook 1 hour to soften veggies.
2. While veggies cook, pan sear chicken breasts with remaining butter.
3. Set chicken to the side and deglaze the pan with remaining chicken stock. Scrape up cooking bits, and add deglazed stock mixture to crockpot.
4. Add thyme, garlic powder, cream cheese, and heavy cream to pot. Stir well to combine.
5. Cut chicken into cubes once cooled and add to pot. Stir in bacon.
6. Set to cook on low 6-8 hours.

Irish Stew

What's in it:

- 4 ounces stout beer
- ¼ C. flour
- 1 ½ C. beef broth
- 3 ounces tomato paste
- ½ tsp. salt
- 2 tsp. steak seasoning blend
- 1 clove of garlic
- ½ white onion
- ½ pound baby carrots
- 1-pound white baby potatoes
- 1 ½ pounds boneless pork shoulder

How it's made:

1. Cut up potatoes and pork into bite-sized chunks and pour into cooker along with carrots.
2. Peel and dice garlic and onion and place into the cooker.
3. Sprinkle with seasonings and pour in beef broth.
4. Whisk flour and water together until a smooth paste is created and dump into the cooker.
5. Stir to incorporate. Then pour in beer.
6. Set to heat on low 8 hours.

Buffalo Chicken Soup

What's in it:

- ¼ C. chopped green onions
- ¼ C. crumbled blue cheese
- ½ C. tortilla chip strips
- 4 C. chicken stock
- ¼ C. blue cheese dressing
- ¼ C. hot cayenne sauce
- 1-pound boneless skinless chicken breast
- 3 sliced celery stalks
- 3 sliced carrots
- 2 minced cloves garlic
- ½ peeled/chopped onion
- 1 tbsp. butter

How it's made:

1. Melt butter in a pan. Then, saute celery, onion, garlic, and carrots together until soft.
2. Pour sautéed veggies into the slow cooker along with chicken stock, blue cheese dressing, cayenne sauce, and chicken breast.
3. Set slow cooker on HIGH and cook for 2 to 3 hours. Or you can set cooker to 24 to 5 hours on low.
4. Remove chicken and shred. Place back into the cooker.
5. Serve topped with tortilla strips, green onions, and crumbled blue cheese.

Chicken Taco Soup

What's in it:

- 1 can pinto beans
- 1 pound boneless skinless chicken breasts
- 3 tbsp. taco seasoning
- 14.5 ounces diced tomatoes
- 15 ounces corn
- 2 C. low-sodium chicken broth
- 1 C. mild salsa
- 1 can black beans

Optional Toppings:

- Tortilla chips
- Green onion
- Avocado
- Grated/shredded cheese
- Sour cream
- Greek yogurt
- Cilantro

How it's made:

1. Pour chicken broth, taco seasoning, diced tomatoes, corn, salsa, pinto and black beans into the cooker. Incorporate well.
2. Place chicken into cooker so that all of the liquid adequately covers the meat.
3. Set to heat on low 6 hours.
4. Take out the chicken. Shred or cut into bite-sized chunks. Then incorporate chicken back into the soup.
5. Serve soup with desired toppings. Enjoy!

Green Chili Enchilada Soup

What's in it:

- Pepper and salt
- 8 ounces softened cream cheese
- 1 tsp. garlic powder
- 1 tsp. onion powder
- 1 tbsp. chili powder
- 2 tbsp. cumin
- ¾ C. water
- 4 ounces diced green chilies
- 15 ounces salsa
- 24 ounces boneless chicken thighs or breasts
- 32 ounces chicken broth

Optional Garnishes:

- Sour cream
- Avocado
- Shredded cheese

How it's made:

1. Put chicken into the base of your cooker.
2. Mix chili powder, garlic powder, cumin, onion powder, cumin, water, green chilies, salsa, and broth together and then pour over chicken.
3. Set to heat on low 7 hours.
4. Take out the chicken and shred with forks. Dump back into the cooker.
5. Add cream cheese and heat half an hour more.
6. Top with desired garnishes when serving.

Creamy Chicken and Gnocchi Soup

What's in it:

- Pepper and salt
- 2 C. baby spinach
- 2/3 C. half and half
- 1 ½ tbsp. flour
- 32 ounces chicken broth
- ¾ - 1 pound chopped rotisserie chicken
- 1 package gnocchi
- ¼ chopped yellow onion
- 3 chopped cloves garlic
- 3 tbsp. butter

How it's made:

1. Melt butter and sauté onion and garlic together for 60 seconds until fragrant. Then pour in chicken, broth, and gnocchi. Heat mixture to boiling point and heat 3 minutes until gnocchi is tenderized.
2. Mix in half and half and flour. Stir until mixture comes up to boiling point again.
3. Remove from heat and add spinach leaves. With pepper and salt, season to reach desired taste. Serve!

White Chicken Chili

What's in it:

- 2 tsp. chili powder
- ½ C. chopped cilantro
- Juice of ½ lime
- 14 ounces full-fat coconut milk
- ¼ tsp. pepper
- 1 tsp. salt
- 2 ½ tsp. cumin
- 6 minced cloves garlic
- 1 diced jalapeno pepper
- 1 bell pepper
- 4 C. chicken broth
- 1 diced onion
- 1 tbsp. avocado oil
- 1 ½ pounds boneless skinless chicken breasts
- 1 tsp. oregano

How it's made:

1. Place spices, garlic, peppers, and onions into the base of your cooker. Put chicken over vegetables, ensuring they are in a singular layer.
2. Add chicken broth over veggies and chicken.
3. Set to heat on low 7-8 hours until chicken is heated thoroughly and veggies become nice and tender.
4. Take out chicken and shred and then dump back in cooker. Set to heat on high. Pour in coconut milk and heat 10-15 minutes until soup is heated thoroughly.
5. Mix in cilantro and lime juice. Taste and season to achieve your desired flavor. Serve with lime wedges and cilantro.

Moroccan Lamb Stew

What's in it:

- 15 ounces chickpeas
- 2 ½ C. beef broth
- 6 halved plum tomatoes
- ½ tsp. ginger
- 1 tsp. Moroccan spice blend
- 1 ½ tsp. allspice
- 1 bay leaf
- 1 cinnamon
- ½ C. dried apricots
- 3 chopped garlic cloves
- 2 ½ pounds boneless leg of lamb
- 6 peeled/cubed Yukon potatoes
- 3 cubed carrots
- 1 chopped yellow onion
- Olive oil

How it's made:

1. In a Dutch oven, warm up 2 tablespoons olive oil and sauté potatoes, carrots, and onions for 4-5 minutes. Then season with pepper, salt, and garlic. Set to the side.
2. Brown lamb while seasoning with pepper and salt. Place sautéed veggies back to pot with lamb. Then pour in bay leaf, spices, cinnamon, and dried apricots, coating well. Add tomatoes and broth and heat to boiling. Heat 5 minutes.
3. Pour all components into a cooker and set to heat on high 3 ½ hours.
4. Serve with pita bread, couscous, or rice. Devour!

Harvest Beef Stew

What's in it:

- Pepper and salt
- 1 tsp. Italian seasoning
- 1 tbsp. balsamic vinegar
- 4 C. water
- 1/3 C. whole wheat flour
- 28-ounce can diced tomatoes
- 4 minced cloves garlic
- 1 chopped onion
- 3 C. russet potatoes
- 3 diced celery ribs
- 2 C. sliced carrots
- 3 tbsp. olive oil
- 1 beef chuck roast
- 2 tbsp. parsley – minced

How it's made:

1. Cut roast into ½-inch chunks. Diced potatoes into ½-inch chunks.
2. Mix flour with beef cubes. Sauté beef 5-10 minutes until browned. Place into slow cooker.
3. Place seasonings, vinegar, water, tomatoes, garlic, onion, potatoes, celery, and carrots to meat in slow cooker. Incorporate well.
4. Set slow cooker to low to cook 5-6 hours. Season with pepper and salt as needed.

Chapter 3: Seafood Soups and Chowders

Slow Cooker Shrimp, Chicken and Sausage Gumbo

What's in it:

- 1 diced green pepper
- 1 1/3 C. heated rice
- 1 tsp. thyme
- 1 tbsp. Cajun spice
- 2 C. chicken broth
- 3 tsp. minced garlic
- 28 ounces diced tomatoes
- 3 diced celery ribs
- 1 hot pepper of choice (habanera, scotch bonnet, Serrano, jalapeno, etc.)
- 1-pound raw/shelled shrimp
- 1 tsp. oregano
- 1-pound smoked sausage of choice (garlic sausage, farmer's sausage, kielbasa, etc.)
- 1-pound chicken breast
- 1 diced onion

How it's made:

1. Place all recipe components into a cooker minus rice and shrimp.
2. Set to heat on low 6-7 hours, ensuring to stir on occasion.
3. In the last hour of cooking, lightly salt shrimp and pour into cooker. During the last 30 minutes, add rice and combine. Heat until rice is heated through.
4. Serve with crusty bread. Enjoy!

Creamy Seafood Chowder

What's in it:

- ¼ tsp. Old Bay seasoning
- ½ pound cooked seafood of choice (crab, lobster tail, shrimp, etc.)
- ½ C. half and half
- ¾ tsp. salt
- 1 chopped potato
- 1-quart seafood stock
- 2 tbsp. all-purpose flour
- 2 minced garlic cloves
- 1 chopped celery stalk
- 1 chopped onion
- 1/8 tsp. cayenne pepper
- 2 chopped carrots
- 2 tbsp. extra virgin olive oil
- ½ tsp. pepper

How it's made:

1. Heat up oil and mix in celery, onion, and carrot, sautéing 3 minutes. Then add garlic and sauté another 60 seconds.
2. Pour flour over veggies and stir. Increase heat and stir in seafood stock.
3. Increase heat to high and let boil. Add potatoes and seasonings. Decrease heat a bit. Cook 8 minutes until potatoes are tender.
4. Mix the seafood the remaining 3 minutes of cooking along with half and half.
5. Taste and season as desired.

San Francisco Seafood Chowder

What's in it:

- 1 tbsp. parsley
- 1-pound mussels
- ½ pound raw shrimp
- ½ pound raw scallops
- ¼ tsp. pepper
- ½ C. diced celery
- 1 bay leaf
- ½ C. diced red bell pepper
- 1 tbsp. lemon juice
- 2 C. water
- ½ C. red wine
- 6 ounces tomato paste
- ½ C. tomatoes
- ½ tsp. salt
- 1 chili pepper
- ½ C. diced carrots
- ½ C. diced leeks
- 2 tbsp. minced garlic
- 1 C. diced onion
- ½ tsp. thyme
- 1 tbsp. olive oil

How it's made:

1. Warm up the oil in a pot. Cook garlic and onion for 5 minutes.
2. Add chili pepper, carrots, bell pepper, celery, and leeks. Cook another 5 minutes. Add tomatoes and cook 3 minutes.
3. Then stir in remaining ingredients. Simmer 25 minutes.

Creamy Tomato Seafood Bisque

What's in it:

- 2 tbsp. flour
- 2-pounds shrimp
- 2 tsp. cooking sherry
- 8-ounces cream cheese
- 2 chopped celery stalks
- 28-ounce can diced tomatoes
- 2 tsp. oregano
- 1 bay leaf
- 1 minced garlic clove
- 1 chopped carrot
- 6 C. chicken broth
- 1 chopped onion
- 5 tbsp. butter

How it's made:

1. Heat butter and add bay leaf and veggies. Cook 10 minutes until tender.
2. Then add flour and stir 1-2 minutes.
3. Pour in broth and add oregano and tomatoes. Heat to boiling, decrease heat and simmer half an hour.
4. Add cream cheese and sherry, cooking 10 minutes.
5. Discard bay leaf. Puree with an emulsion blender.
6. Put back on the stove and add shrimp. Simmer until seafood is cooked.
7. Season to achieve the desired flavor.

Tuscan Seafood Stew

What's in it:

- 2 tbsp. lemon juice
- ¼ pound scallops
- ½ pound shrimp
- 1-pound fish
- 1-pound clams
- ¾ tsp. salt
- 1 C. fish stock
- 14-ounce can chopped tomatoes
- 1 C. white wine
- 1 tbsp. tomato paste
- 1 tbsp. olive oil
- ½ tsp. red pepper flakes
- 5 minced garlic cloves
- 1 chopped onion

How it's made:

1. Pulse pepper flakes, parsley, garlic, and onion in food processor until minced.
2. Heat oil and add minced mixture. Then stir in tomato paste and cook 1 minute.
3. Pour in wine, scraping off bits from the bottom. Bring to boiling and simmer until wine evaporates.
4. Add tomatoes, salt, and stock. Cover and let simmer 10 minutes.
5. Place clams in and cook for 5 minutes.
6. Stir in fish, cook for 5 minutes.
7. Stir in shrimp and scallops and cook 5 minutes.
8. Mix in lemon juice.

New England Clam Chowder

What's in it:

- 2 10-ounce cans minced clams
- 3 tbsp. butter
- 3 C. half and half
- 1 ½ tsp. salt
- 4 C. peeled and cubed potatoes
- 1 ½ C. water
- 4 slices diced bacon
- 1 ½ C. chopped onion

How it's made:

1. Dice bacon and add to a pot, cooking till crispy.
   Add onions to pot with bacon and allow to cook 5 minutes.
   Stir potatoes and water into pot. Season with pepper and salt.
2. Allow mixture to come to a boil. Cook 15 minutes uncovered till potatoes are tenderized.
3. Pour butter and half and half in.
   Drain clams and reserve some of the clam liquid, mixing into soup. Cook 5 minutes till heated thoroughly.

Cajun Shrimp Soup

What's in it:

- ¾ of a pound of shrimp (peeled/deveined)
- ½ C. uncooked long-grain white rice
- Hot pepper sauce
- ½ tsp. salt
- 1 bay leaf
- ¼ tsp. red pepper flakes
- ¼ tsp. dried basil ¼ tsp. dried thyme
- 8-ounces clam juice
- 3 C. tomato-vegetable juice cocktail
- 1 minced garlic clove
- ¼ C. sliced green onions
- ½ C. chopped green bell pepper
- 1 tbsp. butter

How it's made:

1. Melt butter in a pot and sauté garlic, onions, and bell pepper. Then mix in water, clam juice, and veggie juice.
2. Season mixture with salt, bay leaf, red pepper flakes, basil, and thyme.
3. Bring mixture to boiling and mix in rice. Decrease heat and cover, cooking 15 minutes till rice becomes tender.
4. Stir in shrimp and cook another 5 minutes till shrimp is opaque in color.
5. Discard bay leave and season with hot sauce.

Maryland Crab Soup

What's in it:

- 1-gallon water
- 10 steamed blue crab claws
- 1-pound blue crab crabmeat
- 2 C. beef broth
- 2 tbsp. Old Bay seasoning
- 2 tbsp. chopped onion
- 1 C. sliced carrots
- 1 C. frozen corn kernels
- 1 C. lima beans
- 3 C. water
- 2 14.5-ounce cans stewed tomatoes

How it's made:

1. Put beef broth, Old Bay seasoning, onions, sliced carrots, corn, lima beans, water, and tomatoes into pot. Warm to simmering, cover and cook 5 minutes.
2. Boil the gallon of water and add crab claws. Boil 6 minutes. Drain crab and set to the side.
3. Mix crabmeat into vegetable and tomato mixture. Cover and simmer 10 to 15 minutes and serve hot.

Chapter 4: Chilled Soups

Cold Cucumber Dill Soup

What's in it:

- 1 minced garlic clove
- 1-3 tsp. chopped dill
- Juice of 1 lime
- ¼ tsp. cumin
- 2 peeled/sliced cucumber
- 1 minced shallot
- 2 C. Greek yogurt

How it's made:

1. Add all ingredients to a blender.
2. Puree 1 minute until smooth.
3. Adjust seasonings as necessary.
4. Chill at least 1 hour before eating.

Chilled Sweet Corn Soup

What's in it:

- 2 tbsp. salt
- 3-4 cilantro sprigs
- 1 seeded/sliced jalapeno
- 1 C. diced onion
- 2 halved yellow cherry tomatoes
- 2 chopped yellow bell peppers
- 5 ears of fresh corn kernels

How it's made:

1. Toss all ingredients with salt and let sit 1 hour.
2. Place mixture in a blender, pureeing until smooth.
3. Adjust seasonings as needed and drizzle with olive oil.

Curried Zucchini Soup

What's in it:

- 2 tbsp. cilantro
- 1 C. sour cream
- 4 C. vegetable broth
- 2-pounds zucchini
- 2 tsp. curry powder
- 1 minced garlic clove
- 1 chopped onion
- 2 tbsp. olive oil

How it's made:

1. Heat up oil and sauté onion 6-8 minutes. Then add curry powder and garlic, cooking 60 seconds.
2. Increase heat and add salt, broth, and zucchini. Cover and simmer 20 minutes until tender.
3. Puree mixture into small batches in a blender. Chill at least 2 hours.
4. Whisk in pepper, salt, and sour cream right before serving. Garnish with cilantro.

Chapter 5: Grain-Based Soups

Low-Carb Goulash Soup

What's in it:

- 2 cans petite diced tomatoes
- ½ tsp. hot paprika
- 2 tbsp. sweet paprika
- 1 onion
- 4 C. beef stock
- 1 red bell pepper
- 2 tsp. + 1 tsp. olive oil
- 1 ½ - 2 pounds lean ground beef
- 1 tbsp. minced garlic

How it's made:

1. Press SAUTE on instant pot. Heat 2 tablespoons olive oil.
2. Cook ground beef in pot. When browned, take out and put on a plate.
3. When the meat is cooking, cut onion, and red pepper into short strips.
   Pour in 1 teaspoon olive oil into the instant pot after taking out beef.
4. Pour in peppers and onions, cooking 3-4 minutes.
5. Add hot and sweet paprika along with garlic, cooking 2-3 minutes.
6. Pour in beef stock and diced tomatoes, as well as cooked ground beef.
7. Lock lid.
8. Press SOUP and set timer for 15 minutes.
9. Allow pressure to manually release, and then perform a quick release.

10. Serve with a spoonful of sour cream.

Lasagna Soup

What's in it:

- 5-6 basil leaves
- 1 C. shredded mozzarella cheese
- 2 C. beef broth
- 2 14.5-ounce cans fire roasted tomatoes
- ½ C. heavy whipping cream
- 1 C. cottage cheese
- 1 tsp. paprika
- 2 tsp. red pepper flakes
- 1 tbsp. Italian blend herbs
- 1 diced sweet onion
- ½ C. shredded parmesan cheese
- 2 diced garlic cloves
- 1 tbsp. Italian sausage seasoning
- 2-pound ground pork
- 1 tsp. garlic salt

How it's made:

1. Pour seasonings, tomatoes, garlic, onion, and meat into crockpot. Set to cook on high 2 hours.
2. Break up meat.
3. Add cottage cheese to a blender, blending until liquefied. Add to soup.
4. Set to low until you are ready to devour!

Turkey Barley Soup

What's in it:

- 12 C. turkey stock
- 1 C. rinsed barley
- 2 C. heated shredded turkey
- ¼ C. chopped parsley
- 2 C. chopped carrots
- 2 C. sliced celery
- 1 chopped yellow onion

How it's made:

1. Combine turkey stock, barley, turkey, parsley, carrots, celery, and onion within your cooker.
2. Set heat to low to cook 6 to 7 hours or set to heat to high to cook for 4 hours.
3. Serve while hot and sprinkle with additional parsley.

Black Bean Soup

What's in it:

- ½ tsp. cayenne pepper
- 2 tsp. chili powder
- 4 15-ounce cans black beans
- 4 C. vegetable stock
- 1-2 jalapeno peppers
- 2 tsp. cumin
- 5 minced cloves garlic
- 2 chopped carrots
- 2 chopped red bell peppers
- 1 chopped onion
- 2 tsp. salt

Optional Toppings:

- Shredded cheese
- Sour cream
- Avocados
- Crumbled tortilla chips
- Cilantro

How it's made:

1. Drain black beans, chop, and de-seed jalapeno peppers.
2. Mix all ingredients in your slow cooker.
3. Set slow cooker to cook 6 to 8 hours on low. Or set to high to cook 6 to 8 hours. You want veggies to be tenderized.
4. You can serve as is or pour into a food processor to blend until you reach desired consistency.
5. Top with desired toppings when serving.

Spiced Carrot and Lentil Soup

What's in it:

- 1 C. milk
- ½ C. vegetable stock
- ¾ C. split red lentils
- 4 C. washed/chopped carrot s
- 2 tbsp. olive oil
- Pinch of chili flakes
- 2 tsp. cumin seeds

How it's made:

1. Dump all recipe components into your slow cooker.
2. Place cooker to cook 5 hours on low heat until carrots become softened.
3. With an immersion blender, blend soup until creamy and smooth.

Chicken and Rice Soup

What's in it:

- 9 C. chicken broth
- 3 chopped celery stalks
- 2 tbsp. butter
- 1 bay leaf
- ½ tsp. sage
- ½ tsp. rosemary
- 2 tsp. parsley
- 3 tsp. salt
- Pepper
- 3 minced cloves garlic
- 3 chopped carrots
- 1 C. brown rice
- 3 chicken breasts (cut in half and trimmed of fat)
- 1 chopped onion

How it's made:

1. Pour all recipe components into your cooker, minus the rice.
2. Set to heat on low for 4 hours. Add rice halfway through the heating cycle.
3. Half an hour before preparing to serve, take out chicken and shred. Place chicken back into slow heat and heat 30 minutes.

Slow Cooker Chicken Noodle Soup

What's in it:

- 1 tbsp. lemon juice
- ¼ C. chopped parsley
- 2 C. unheated egg noodles
- 3 tbsp. extra-virgin olive oil
- Pepper and salt
- 2 bay leaves
- ¼ tsp. crushed celery seed
- ½ tsp. sage
- ½ tsp. rosemary
- ¾ tsp. thyme
- 1 C. water
- 6 C. chicken broth
- 3-5 minced cloves garlic
- 1 chopped yellow onion
- 5 chopped carrots
- 1 ½ pounds boneless skinless chicken thighs or breasts
- 4 stalks chopped celery

How it's made:

1. Place garlic, celery, onion, carrots, and chicken in the cooker. Then add bay leaves, celery seeds, rosemary, thyme, water, broth, and olive oil. Season with pepper and salt.
2. Set to heat on low 6-7 hours.
3. Take out the chicken and let sit 10 minutes. Cut chicken into bite sizes. Place parsley and egg noodles into cooker and heat 10 more minutes.
4. Mix in lemon juice and return chicken to cooker. Stir to combine.

5. Serve topped with parmesan cheese and with saltine crackers.

Sausage, Spinach, and White Bean Soup

What's in it:

- 3 C. baby spinach leaves
- Pepper and salt
- 4 C. chicken broth
- 2 bay leaves
- ½ tsp. oregano
- 2 15-ounce cans great northern beans
- 2 diced stalks celery
- 3 diced carrots
- 1 diced onion
- 3 minced cloves of garlic
- 1 package andouille sausage
- 1 tbsp. olive oil

How it's made:

1. Warm up olive oil. Thinly slice sausage and add to pan, cooking 3-4 minutes until just browned.
2. Pour bay leaves, oregano, beans, celery, carrots, onions, garlic, and sausage into slow cooker. Mix in 2 cups of water along with chicken broth. Season with pepper and salt.
3. Adjust the timer on the cooker to cook for 7 hours on low or 3 to 4 hours on high.
4. Stir in spinach until it becomes wilted.

Spicy Grain Soup

What's in it:

- ½ C. salted roasted pumpkin seeds
- 1 diced parsnip
- 1 diced zucchini
- 1 diced carrot
- 15-ounce can black beans
- ½ a pound mushrooms
- 1 tsp. allspice
- 6 sprigs cilantro
- 1 ½ C. canned diced tomatoes
- 2 quarts vegetable broth
- 2 halved cloves garlic
- 1 sliced onion
- 3 dried chilies
- 1 tbsp. olive oil
- ½ C. bulgur
- ½ C. short-grain brown rice
- Water
- ½ C. pearl barley

How it's made:

1. Pour barley into 4 cups of water and heat to boiling. Simmer 35 minutes until tender. Drain and return to pan.
2. Pour rice into 2 cups of water and heat to boiling. Simmer 35 minutes until tender and drain. Add to cooked barley.
3. Pour bulgur into 1 cup of hot water. Let stand 10 minutes until bulgur absorbs the liquid.
4. Warm up olive oil. Add garlic, onions, and chilies to oil and brown 5 minutes. Then add allspice, cilantro, tomatoes, and broth, seasoning with pepper and salt.

5. Heat to boiling and let simmer 45 minutes.
6. Allow to cool a bit before pureeing. Return to pan.
7. Add parsnip, zucchini, carrot, black beans, and mushrooms. Bring to a boil and simmer 20 minutes. Then add bulgur, rice, and barley.
Season with pepper and salt.
8. Ladle into serving bowls and sprinkle with pumpkin seeds and cilantro.

Greens and Grains Soup

What's in it:

- 6 C. vegetable stock
- 2 minced garlic cloves
- 1 tbsp. extra virgin olive oil
- 10 ounces greens of choice (Swiss chard, kale, bok choy, spinach, etc.)
- 2 tsp. sea salt
- 1 C. whole grains of choice (brown rice, wheat berries, spelt, farro, barley, etc.)

How it's made:

1. Rinse choice of grain and pour into pot with sea salt and just enough water to cover. Heat to boiling and let simmer until just tender.
2. Cut stalks and leave from greens and finely chop up.
3. Warm up oil in a soup pot and add green stalks. Cook 5 minutes until softened.
4. Add garlic and stir well. Then add veggie stock, cooking until mixture is almost boiling. Add greens and combine well, cooking 1-2 minutes until wilted.
5. Season with pepper and salt.
6. Ladle into soup bowls.

Conclusion

I want to congratulate you on making it to the end of *The Complete Soup Maker Cookbook.*

As you have read, there are soup recipes that can suit your everyday needs all day long! Whether you are feeling something hearty, chilly, seafood, or deluxe, there is a soup recipe in this book to fulfill your desires and satisfy your taste buds, all the while being kind to your waste!
I hope that whatever your goals may be when it comes to your health that you will find this soup recipe cookbook to be helpful as you learn how important it is to regain lost time and remaster a healthier lifestyle.

The next step? Try out some of the soup recipes that caught your eye! There is no reason to wait, be soup-tastic starting today!

The Complete Vegetarian Recipes Cookbook

Chapter 1: Quick and Tasty Vegetarian Breakfast Recipes

Looking for quick, healthy and delicious on the go or leisurely breakfast options? We've got you covered with these fantastic bunch of delicious breakfast/brunch ideas that are fast, scrumptious and easy to make.

1. Tofu and Gorgonzola Scramble

Time: 20 Minutes

Ingredients:

- ¼ cup red onion (chopped)
- 2/3 cup white mushrooms (sliced)
- 4 tablespoons Gorgonzola cheese (crumbled /grated)
- 1 garlic clove (minced)
- 2 tablespoons olive oil
- 12-ounce firm tofu (cubed)
- 1 cup spinach

Method:

1. Heat skillet. Add olive oil.
2. Add onion, garlic, tofu until onion turns translucent.
3. Add mushrooms and cook until they turn soft for 5-7 minutes. Tofu should be slightly brownish.
4. Remove from heat. Combine spinach and cheese, and add to the tofu mixture until the Gorgonzola cheese melts and the spinach starts wilting.

2. Avocado and Goat Cheese Toast

Time: 10 Minutes

Ingredients:

- Ingredients:
- 4 slices bread (crusty)
- ½ cup goat cheese (crumbled or grated)
- Red pepper flakes
- Extra virgin olive oil
- One ripe avocado
- Sea salt

Method:

1. Toast bread until it turns light brown and crunchy.
2. Mash avocado and divide equally into four parts.
3. Sprinkle grated goat cheese.
4. Add olive oil, followed by pepper flakes and salt.

3. Veggie Pita Pizza

Time: 25 minutes

Ingredients:

- 1 clove garlic (crushed, minced)
- ½ cup bell pepper (diced)
- ½ cup baby mushrooms (sliced)
- ½ cup red onion (diced)
- 1 cup spinach (roughly chopped)
- Hot sauce (as per taste)
- Black pepper (as per taste)
- 2 tablespoons Greek yogurt
- 1 ½ tablespoon sriracha sauce
- ½ cup cheese (shredded)
- Olive Oil for spraying
- Water (cooking)
- 1 pita bread (whole wheat)
- 1 egg (beaten)

Method:

1. Preheat oven to 180 degrees C. Add cooking spray on a medium sized .baking sheet.
2. Add little water to a skillet and heat until it turns very hot. Add garlic, mushrooms red onions, and pepper and keep cooking for 8 minutes or until mixture turns soft and mushy. Combine water as necessary.
3. Combine spinach and cook for a couple of minutes until it wilts.
4. Beat the egg, fiery sauce, and black pepper. Add to the vegetable mixture on the skillet and cook until the egg is completely scrambled on medium heat.
5. Bake the pita for 4-5 minutes until it turns golden brown.
6. Mix yogurt and sriracha, and combine well.

7. Spread yogurt and sriracha sauce on pita bread and add egg and veggie mixture.
8. Sprinkle cheese on top.
9. Cook for 4 minutes or until cheese goes gooey.
10. Cut into slices and serve.

4. Focaccia Tomato Basil Sandwiches

Time: 30 minutes

Ingredients

- (2 sandwiches)
- 1 yellow bell pepper (use roasted ones from the deli when you are short of time)
- 2 tbsps. sundried tomato puree
- 4 ripe halved ripe tomatoes
- One half of big focaccia bread
- 1 tbsp. olive oil
- 4 oz. (110 g) mozzarella sliced
- 8 basil leaves
- Ground pepper and table salt (as per taste)

Method:

1. Preheat broiler. Line pan with foil.
2. Grill peppers until blistered.
3. Wrap the pepper in foil to seal it and allow it to cool.
4. Cut the focaccia vertically half, and horizontally into quarters. Toast on both sides in the broiler.
5. Spread sun-dried tomato puree on both sides.
6. Line broiler with foil and place tomatoes on it. Drizzle with olive oil. Cook for 4-5 minutes until tomatoes have turned mushy. Sprinkle salt and pepper.
7. Cut pepper into strips and add pepper slices and tomatoes to the focaccia. Sprinkle mozzarella cheese and basil

leaves. Drizzle oil from pan. Place the other half focaccia bread and serve warm.

5. Tasty Veggie Tacos

Time: 20-25 minutes (3 tacos)

Ingredients for filling

- 1 ½ garlic cloves (minced)
- Half zucchini (sliced into thin strips)
- Half red pepper (chopped)
- Half white onion (diced)
- ½ lime (juice)
- Salt, pepper flakes and black pepper ground (as per taste)
- 3 eggs (scrambled)
- 4-5 cherry tomatoes (chopped)
- 1 teaspoon olive oil
- 3 small to mid-sized tortillas
- Choice of garnishing – feta cheese, hot sauce, jalapeno, etc.

Method:

1. Heat skillet. When sufficiently heated, add olive oil.
2. Add onions and salt and cook until onions turn translucent for 5 minutes.
3. Introduce garlic and pepper flakes and sauté for 45 seconds to a minute.
4. Add zucchini and bell pepper until the mixture has gone soft for 5-7 minutes. We need a softened mixture not runny/mushy one.
5. Turn off heat and add lime juice. Add salt, stir well and set aside.
6. Scramble eggs and add hot sauce, black pepper, and salt. Cook on medium heat.

7. Fold in cherry tomatoes and set aside the mixture.
8. Warm tortilla on medium heat. Remove aside on a plate. Top it with eggs and veggie mixture. Garnish with feta, hot sauce, jalapeno, etc.

6. Tasty Tofu Burritos

Time: 15 minutes

Ingredients (2 burritos)

- 2 big mushrooms (sliced)
- 1 clove garlic (diced)
- ¼ cup red onion (diced)
- ½ package extra firm tofu (crumbled/grated)
- ¼ tsp of cumin, salt, pepper, turmeric, chili powder, garlic powder each mixed with 1 ½ tsp water.
- 2 wraps
- Lime juice 1tspn
- Lettuce (2 leaves)
- Sliced avocado (1 cup)
- Refried beans (1 cup)
- Salsa (as per taste)
- Cilantro leaves

Method:

1. Heat pan sufficiently
2. Introduce diced garlic, red pepper, mushrooms and onion and cook for about 10 minutes until the mixture turns soft and mushy.
3. Add tofu and the entire spices mixture into the pan.
4. Stir and cook until tofu is hot.
5. You can either heat refried beans separately or add them cold.

6. Add generous heaps of beans, cilantro, lettuce, avocado, lime juice and salsa to the wraps. Fill the tofu mixture.
7. Wrap and enjoy.

7. Fiery Baked Tomatoes and Eggs

Time: 25 minutes

Ingredients (serves 2)

- 2 tbsps. olive oil
- 1 red chili (deseed and chop finely)
- Coriander bunch small (chopped)
- 3 small red onions (chopped)
- 1 garlic clove
- 4 eggs
- 1 tsp castor sugar
- Cherry tomato cans (2 400 gm each)

Method:

1. Heat pan (with a lid). Slowly add oil. Add onions, garlic, chopped coriander and red chili for 5-10 minutes until the mixture softens. Combine tomatoes and castor sugar.
2. Allow the mixture to bubble for 10 minutes until it thickens.
3. The mixture can be frozen and stored for a month.
4. Use a large spoon to make four crevices in the sauce. Crack open an egg into each of the four openings. Cover and keep cooking on low to medium heat for 8-10 minutes until the eggs are done as per your preference.
5. Sprinkle some coriander leaves. Serve with warm crusty bread.

8. Pesto Toast

Time: 20 minutes

Ingredients: (2 toasts)

- ¼ cup hulled pumpkin seeds
- 1 medium clove garlic
- 1 big avocado
- Salt (as per taste)
- Basil leaves (1/3 cup)
- 1 tbsp. lemon juice

Optional accompaniments include cherry tomatoes, ground black pepper, and pepper flakes.

1. Add pumpkin seeds to a skillet and cook on slow to medium heat. Cook until the seeds crackle and make popping sounds. Remove from flame and set aside to cool.
2. Pit the avocados into two by scooping out its insides into a food processor. Add lemon juice, garlic, and salt as per taste. Blend until mixture turns smooth.
3. Add pumpkin seeds and basil to pulse the entire mixture until it is finely blended. Add more salt if necessary.
4. Toast bread, and spread a generous heap of avocado pesto on each slice. Serve with tomatoes. Top it with ground pepper and red pepper flakes. Serve hot.

9. Green Hummus (With Toast or Pita)

Time: 20 minutes

Ingredients (Approx. 2 cups)

- ¼ cup tahini
- 2 tablespoons olive oil (keep more aside for drizzling on top)
- ½ cup fresh parsley (chopped)
- ¼ cup lemon juice
- ½ cup fresh tarragon (roughly chopped)
- Salt (as per taste)
- 1 garlic clove (chopped)
- One can of chickpeas (washed and drained)
- 3 tbsps. fresh chives (chopped)
- Fresh herbs for garnishing

Method:

1. Combine tahini and lemon juice into a creamy, smooth mixture. Whip it first before adding to a food processor.
2. Add olive oil, chives, garlic, tarragon, parsley and salt to the mixture and processes it again. Pause to scrape mixture from the bowl when necessary.
3. Add half the given quantity of chickpeas and process for a minute or two. Slowly add remainder chickpeas and process until mixture is smooth yet thick. Add water slowly if the mixture is too lumpy and process until you achieve the desired consistency.
4. Remove mixture in a bowl. Drizzle 1 teaspoon of olive oil.
5. Serve with pita bread or crusty bread or toast.
6. Refrigerate in a container and use as required until a week.

10. Savory Quinoa Bowl

Time: 15 minutes

Ingredients (single serving)

- 100 gm extra firm tofu (crumbled)
- ¼ cup cherry tomatoes
- 1 cup kale (tear into tiny pieces)
- ½ cup carrot (grated)
- ½ cup mushrooms (sliced)
- ½ teaspoon garlic powder
- ½ cup broccoli (chopped)
- ½ teaspoon curry powder (yellow)
- ½ teaspoon paprika
- ½ teaspoon onion powder
- Salt and pepper (as per taste)
- Half a lime
- ½ cup quinoa (cooked)
- ½ avocado (sliced)
- ½ cup sprouts (deli)

Method:

1. Heat a wok over high heat.
2. Combine spices and seasonings in a large bowl and keep aside.
3. When the wok is sufficiently heated, add mushrooms, carrot, and broccoli with a few drops of water. Cook for about 6-7 minutes until vegetables turn mushy.
4. Reduce heat and combine cherry tomatoes, spice mixture, and kale. Continue to stir and cook until the kale wilts. Keep splashing water to prevent the mixture from sticking, burning or overcooking.
5. Add lime juice and tofu until it scrambles into the mixture and turns golden brown.
6. Add the mixture to a quinoa bowl.

7. Sprinkle the entire mixture with sprouts and/or sliced avocado. Add more lime, salt, and pepper if required.

11. Chickpea Omelet

Time: 15 Minutes

Ingredients (for 3 small sized omelets)

- 1 cup chickpea flour
- ½ teaspoon each of onion, garlic, white pepper and black pepper powder
- 1/3 cup yeast
- ½ teaspoon baking soda
- 4 ounces mushrooms (sautéed)
- 3 green onions (chopped)

Method:

1. Mix chickpea flour, garlic powder, onion powder, black pepper and white pepper, yeast and baking soda in a bowl. Add some water to make a smooth batter.
2. Heat pan sufficiently. Pour batter into the pan and spread evenly. Add a couple of tablespoons of mushrooms and green onions for cooking each omelet. Keep flipping it periodically until both sides are cooked evenly.
3. Top your omelet with spinach, hot sauce, salsa, tomatoes and any other topping of your choice.

Chapter 2: Quick and Easy Vegetarian Lunch Recipes

1. Egg Fried Cauliflower

Ingredients (2 servings)

- 2 tbsps. coconut oil
- Slices of yellow, red and green (diced)
- A small onion (diced)
- Cherry tomatoes (half punnet)
- 1 full head cauliflower (grated). To save time, you can use premade Tesco ones
- ½ Peas (fresh or frozen)
- 2 beaten eggs
- Salt and black pepper (as per taste)
- Optional - Soya sauce (use tamari soya sauce if you are looking for a gluten-free alternative)

Method:

1. Heat oil in a large wok. Add onion and peppers and cook for 2-3 minutes.
2. Add tomatoes and peas. Fry this mixture for another 3 minutes.
3. Combine beaten eggs with the vegetables and spread evenly, so the vegetable mixture is completely covered. Spread evenly instead of stirring. Wait for a minute before mixing the eggs to form a scrambled preparation.
4. Add cauliflower and sauté for another 5-7 minutes till the mixture turns soft.
5. Season with soya sauce, salt, and pepper.

Tip – This mixture can make for scrumptious wrap fillings or can be eaten by itself as a quick, easy and delicious lunch option.

2. Greek Nachos

Time: 20 Minutes

Ingredients (3 servings)

- ½ tablespoon lemon juice
- Fresh ground pepper (as per taste)
- ½ cup lettuce (chopped)
- 1 ½ cups whole grain pita chips
- ¼ cup grape tomatoes (quartered)
- ¼ cup feta cheese (crumbled)
- 1 tablespoon olives (Kalamata chopped)
- 1 tablespoon red onion (chopped)
- ½ cup hummus
- ½ tablespoon oregano for seasoning
- 1 tbsp. olive oil

Method

1. Mix hummus (leave some aside), olive oil, pepper and lemon juice.
2. Arrange a layer of pita on a plate. Dollop hummus on the chips.
3. Add lettuce, feta cheese, olives, red onions, and tomatoes. Add a dollop of the hummus mixture set aside in a bowl. Top off with oregano.

3. Delicious Thai Noodle Soup

Ingredients (2 bowls)

- ½ packet or 4-ounce rice vermicelli noodles
- ½ freshly peeled and crushed ginger
- 1 ½ cups vegetable stock (without salt)
- ½ cup carrots (thinly sliced)
- ½ red pepper (thinly sliced)
- 2 garlic cloves (crushed)
- Half cucumber (thinly sliced lengthwise)
- 2 ½ tablespoons fresh herbs (mixed)
- 3 tablespoons roasted peanuts without salt
- 1 teaspoon chili oil
- 1 ½ low sodium soy sauce

Method:

1. Cook noodles as mentioned on the packet and drain.
2. Heat pan sufficiently. Slowly add oil. Throw in ginger and garlic to cook for about 1-2 minutes, continuously stirring the mixture.
3. Introduce stock and low sodium soy sauce. Let it boil while stirring continuously.
4. Simmer mixture for 10-12 minutes.
5. Add cucumber, carrots, and pepper in a bowl and combine nicely. Portion out noodles into two serving bowls.
6. Top each bowl with half the vegetable mixture.
7. Pour half of the stock into each bowl.
8. Sprinkle with peanuts and herbs.
9. Drizzle with some chili oil for added flavor.

4. Nuts Fried Rice

Ingredients (3 servings)

- 1 ½ tablespoons sesame oil
- 1 ½ cups broccoli florets
- 1 package pre-made brown rice
- 4 ounces sliced shiitake mushrooms
- ½ cup roasted cashews (not salted)
- 1 beaten egg
- 1 ½ tablespoon low sodium soy sauce
- ¼ cup peanut butter
- ¼ teaspoons black pepper
- ½ tablespoon rice vinegar
- ½ tablespoon water
- ½ tablespoon sesame seeds (toasted)

Method:

1. Heat ½ tablespoon oil on a high flame in a large nonstick skillet.
2. Add mushrooms and broccoli. Continue cooking for 5-7 more minutes. Turn off heat and set aside.
3. Add rest of the 1 tablespoon of oil. Introduce rice along with nuts. Cook for another 7-8 minutes.
4. Combine eggs to cook for a couple of minutes until they are well cooked.
5. Add broccoli, half a tablespoon of soy sauce and pepper.
6. Add remaining 1 ½ tablespoon soy sauce, vinegar, peanut butter, and half a tablespoon of water in a bowl. Top rice with peanut butter mix and sprinkle sesame seeds for extra taste.

5. Delicious Panzanella Salad (Light Bread and Tomatoes Italian Salad)

Time: 20 minutes
Ingredients (one large bowl)

- 3 tbsps. olive oil
- 2 large tomatoes (ripe and cubed)
- 1 yellow pepper (cubed)
- 15 basil leaves (chopped)
- 1 cucumber (sliced into ½ inch slices)
- ½ red onion (sliced thinly)

Dressing:

- 1 tsp garlic (crushed)
- 1/2 cup oil olive
- ½ tsp Dijon mustard
- 3 1/2 tbsps. capers
- ¼ tsp fresh ground black pepper
- Salt (as per taste)
- 3 ½ tbsps. wine vinegar

Method:

1. Make the dressing by combining garlic, vinegar, olive oil (half quantity), mustard, salt, and pepper.
2. Add rest of the olive oil to a pan. Cook bread cubes on low heat for 8-10 minutes until they turn golden brown.
3. Add more olive oil as required.
4. Mix cucumber, bell pepper, red onion, tomato, capers and basil in a big bowl.
5. Add the vinaigrette along with cooked bread cubes to it and toss.
6. Combine seasoning (salt and pepper)

6. Baba Ghanoush

Time: 15 minutes
Ingredients (2 bowls)

- 4 small aubergines
- Salt and pepper (as per taste)
- garlic cloves (chopped roughly)
- 3 tbsps. parsley (chopped)
- 2 pinches red chili powder
- 4 tbsps. tahini paste
- 40 ml lemon juice
- 2 tbsps. olive oil (optional for drizzle)

Method:

1. Peel aubergines and add its flesh to a processor along with other ingredients.
2. Blend until you get a smooth mixture.
3. Season with salt, pepper, chili powder, parsley and olive oil (optional).
4. Enjoy with pita bread.

7. Easy Veggie Muffins

Time: 20 minutes

Ingredients (4 servings)

- 4 Muffins (Toasted English ones)
- 1 cup alfalfa sprouts
- 1 small onion (chopped)
- 1 avocado (mashed)
- 1 tomato (chopped)
- 5 tbsps. salad dressing (ranch style)
- 1 cup cheddar cheese (smoked)
- 5 tbsps. well toasted black sesame seeds

Method:

1. Begin by preheating oven on the broil mode.
2. Put a muffin on the cookie sheet open after splitting.
3. Spread every half with avocado by portioning all ingredients evenly. Cover every half with tomatoes, cheese, onion, sprouts, dressing and sesame seeds.
4. Broil until cheese melts into a golden brown and bubbles.

8. Light and Delicious Pasta Salad

Time: 20 minutes
Ingredients (serves 4-6)

Method:

- 1/2 box tri-colored pasta
- 1 ½ cup red onions (chopped)
- 1/2 lb. sliced cottage cheese
- ½ lb. provolone cheese (cubed)
- 1 ½ cup green pepper
- ½ cup black olives (sliced)
- 1 cup tomatoes (diced)

Dressing

- ¾ cup extra virgin olive oil
- 1 tablespoon oregano
- ¾ cup wine vinegar
- Salt and pepper
- ¾ cup sugar

Method:

1. Combine all salad dressing ingredients and keep it aside.
2. Prepare pasta as per box instructions.
3. Add cottage cheese slices.
4. Mix cottage cheese, chopped ingredients with cooked pasta.
5. Add dressing and chill for a while if you want a cold salad. If you like a more moist salad texture, pour additional olive oil or vinegar.
6. Top with cheese before serving.

9. Mexican Guacamole with Tortilla

Time: 20 minutes
Ingredients (2-3 servings)

- 2 ½ Roma tomatoes (diced)
- 3 avocados (peeled and mashed)
- ½ cup onion (finely chopped)
- 1 tsp garlic (minced)
- 3 tbsps. fresh cilantro (chopped)
- 1/2 lime juice

Method:

1. Combine lime juice, salt, pepper and mashed avocados.
2. Add onion, cilantro, garlic, and onion.
3. Add more pepper if required.
4. Refrigerate to serve cold or serve immediately
5. The versatile guacamole can eaten by itself as a salad or combined with tortillas or even as a wrap filling for quick, easy and delicious lunches.

10. Parmesan Spinach Baked Rice

Time: 30 minutes
Ingredients (2 servings)

- 1 package frozen spinach (chopped). Ensure excess water is removed from it.
- 2 ½ cups cooked rice
- 2 cups cheese (grated)
- 1 cup parmesan cheese (crumbled)
- 1/2 cup butter
- 2 big green onions (chopped)
- 1 garlic clove (minced)
- ¾ cup milk
- 3 big eggs (beaten)
- Salt and pepper (as per taste)
- ¼ cup parmesan for garnishing
- Mozzarella grated (optional garnish)

Method:

1. Preheat oven to 180 degrees C and lightly drizzle medium-sized baking dish.
2. Combine butter, cheddar cheese, rice, onions, eggs, milk, parmesan cheese, spinach and garlic until it is fully combined.
3. Add salt and pepper as per taste.
4. Place the mixture on the baking dish and garnish with parmesan.
5. Bake for 20 minutes. If you're garnishing with mozzarella, add it during the last 3-4 minutes of the baking time.

11. Mexican Pico De Gallo

Time: 15 Minutes
Ingredients (2 servings)

- 2-3 Jalapeno peppers (sliced)
- ½ tbsp. lime juice
- 4 fully ripe plum tomatoes (roughly chopped)
- 1 white onion (diced)
- Salt (as per taste)
- 1 cup coriander (roughly chopped)

Method:

1. Mix all ingredients and cover.
2. Refrigerate if you want to enjoy it cold. Otherwise, it is good to go as it is. Avoid storing it and consume on the same day for freshness.

12. Super Vegetarian Club Sandwich

Time: 10 minutes
Ingredients (serves 1)

- 3 slices large granary bread
- Lemon juice (one squeeze)
- 1 carrot (peel and grate coarsely)
- 2 tomatoes (sliced thickly)
- 1 tbsp. olive oil
- 2 tbsps. hummus
- 1 handful of watercress

Method:

1. Toast bread lightly. In the meantime, mix carrot, lemon juice, olive oil, and watercress.
2. Spread hummus on each toast slice.
3. Add watercress and carrot mixture to one slice. Put another slice on top of it and top it with a thick tomato slice. Finally, add the third slice (hummus side will be down).
4. Cut sandwich into quarters and enjoy.

13. Tomato Mozzie Burger

Time: 10 Minutes
Ingredients (serves 3)

- 3 large ripened tomatoes
- Salt and pepper (as per taste)
- 4 ounces mozzarella (unsalted)
- 1 tbsp. olive oil
- ½ large garlic clove (sliced thinly)
- 1 sprig fresh basil leaves

Method:

1. Heat oven at 450 degrees F. Cut the tomato into two horizontal halves. You may have to cut the bottom of the tomato to make it stand properly.
2. Arrange tomatoes with the cut portion up on a foil-lined baking sheet (rimmed) or roasting pan.
3. Cover with oil. Add seasoning as required. Sprinkle thinly sliced garlic over tomatoes.
4. Roast until it is softened for around 12-15 minutes.
5. In the meantime, cut mozzarella into three ½ inch slices. Use a spatula to sandwich the slice between two warm tomato halves until the heat slightly melts the mozzarella.
1. Drizzle tomatoes with all the accumulated juices in the pan and garnish with fresh basil before serving.

14. Israeli Salad

Time- 15 Minutes
Ingredients (4 servings)

- 1/2 lb. cucumbers (Persian or other variants diced)
- 1/3 cup onion (chopped, minced)
- ½ lb. fresh fully ripe tomatoes (sliced)
- ½ cup fresh parsley (minced)
- Sal (as per taste)
- 1 ½ tbsps. extra virgin oil olive
- 1 ½ fresh lemon juice

Method:

1. Combine diced cucumbers with all ingredients.
2. Combine well until the veggies combine with oil, fresh parsley, salt and lemon juice.
3. Tastes best at room temperature, though you can refrigerate if you prefer a more chilled version. Enjoy as a salad or a healthy, light lunch.

Chapter 3: Simple and Delicious Vegetarian Dinners

1. African Sweet Potatoes in Peanut Soup

Time: 25 minutes
Ingredients (2-3 servings)

- ½ tsp peanut oil
- 1 ½ garlic clove (crushed)
- 2 c low sodium vegetable broth
- ¼ can tomatoes (diced)
- ½ onion (finely chopped)
- 1-inch ginger (finely chopped)
- 1 lb. sweet potatoes (peel and cut into one-inch chunky pieces)
- ½ c peanut butter
- ½ tbsp. tomato paste
- ½ tsp cayenne (depending on taste you can add or reduce quantity)
- 1 c collard greens
- Salt as per taste
- Toasted peanuts for garnish

Method:

1. Heat peanut oil in soup pot. Add garlic, ginger, sweet potatoes and onion. Cook on medium flame until the mixture softens.
2. Add tomatoes, cayenne, tomato paste, peanut butter, and broth. Keep stirring to mix ingredients well until it begins to simmer.
3. Simmer on low heat for 8-10 minutes by covering the pot.
4. Coarsely mash the potatoes with a masher.

5. Add greens and simmer without covering the pot for 3-4 minutes.
6. Add salt as per taste.
7. Serve on a bed of brown taste.
8. Garnish with toasted peanuts.

2. Dutch Mosterdsoep Soup

Time: 20 minutes
Ingredients (2-3 servings)

- 3 cups vegetable stock
- ½ cup flour
- 3 tbsps. mustard
- ¼ cup butter
- 1 tbsps. whipped cream
- Salt and pepper (as per taste)

Method:

1. Add vegetable stock to pan. Bring to boil while stirring.
2. In another pan, melt butter and add flour. Keep stirring to avoid formations of lumps. Cook until you get a smooth mixture and for about 4-5 minutes.
3. Add stock gradually at about 1/4th cup each time. Stir continuously. Cook continuously till mixture has an even and creamy consistency, without lumps.
4. Simmer on low heat after adding entire stock for 12 minutes.
5. Add whipped cream on top and serve hot.

3. Rice and Tofu Filled Peppers (a delicious vegetarian twist on a classic beef recipe)

Time: 30 minutes
Ingredients (4 portions)

- 2 cups cooked brown or white rice
- 2 ½ cups marinara sauce
- 1 garlic clove (finely chopped)
- 3 tbsps. olive oil
- 2 red bell peppers (cut into halves)
- 4 slices of tomato
- 2 cups mozzarella cheese (shredded)
- 1 packet of extra firm tofu (diced after draining)
- 2 yellow bell peppers (cut into halves)
- Salt and pepper

Method:

1. Heat oil in a skillet and cook on low heat. Introduce tofu and finely chopped garlic and keep cooking for around 5-6 minutes.
2. Mix a 1 cup of marinara sauce.
3. Add salt and pepper as per taste and cook until mixture turns golden brown.
4. Preheat oven to 175 degrees c.
5. Add equal portions of rice into each of the peppers. Add remaining marinara sauce and a cup of cheese.
6. Add tofu, again equally portioned into 4 peppers.
7. Place sliced tomato on each pepper and garnish with the remaining cup of cheese.
8. Bake peppers for 20 minutes till the cheese melts. Serve hot.

4. Thai Peanut Vegetarian Pasta

Time: 25 Minutes
Ingredients (2 servings)

- 1 red onion (thin half circular slices)
- ½ large carrot (cut into thin sticks)
- ½ tbsp. grated ginger
- 1 clove garlic
- 8 ounces cremini mushrooms (sliced)
- 1 tbsp. olive oil
- ½ large bell pepper (sliced)
- 3 tbsps. soy sauce
- 1 tbsp. peanut butter
- 4 ounces whole wheat spaghetti
- ½ lime juice
- ¼ cilantro (chopped)
- ¼ peanuts (chopped)
- 1 ½ tbsps. rice vinegar

Method:

1. Heat olive oil in a skillet on low flame. Introduce onion, carrots, and mushrooms. Cook continuously for 7 minutes or until the mixture turns soft. Add ginger, garlic, and pepper. Sauté for 2-3 minutes.
2. Mix soya sauce, peanut butter, and rice vinegar. Add this mixture to the skillet. Pour in the broth slowly. Stir and mix.
3. Add spaghetti and cook until it softens. Increase heat, cover skillet and bring to boil.
4. Remove cover and lower heat. Cook for 9-10 minutes or until the pasta gets semi cooked or al Dante. It should absorb the liquid. Keep stirring.

5. Garnish with cilantro, lime juice, and chopped peanuts.

5. Spicy Vegetarian Tikka Masala

Time: 25 minutes
Ingredients (5 servings)

- 1 tsp turmeric (ground)
- ¼ tsp red pepper (crushed)
- 2 packages 14 ounces each of extra firm tofu
- 2 tbsps. canola oil
- 1 ½ large bell pepper (sliced)
- 1 tbsp. ginger (minced)
- 1 ½ large onion (sliced)
- 28-ounce can of sundried tomatoes
- 1 tbsp. flour
- 2 garlic cloves (crushed)

Method:

1. Mix garam masala, salt, turmeric and red pepper (can be skipped if you want to avoid extra spice in a bowl.
2. Add one inch cubed tofu pieces in a bowl with a tablespoon of spice mix.
3. Heat 1 tablespoon oil on low flame. Throw in tofu. Keep cooking it for 10-12 minutes, stirring occasionally until tofu turns golden brown. Transfer mix on plate.
4. Add remaining oil, onion, ginger, garlic, bell pepper and keep cooking the mixture, until it gets browned in 5 minutes.
5. Add flour along with remaining spice mix. Let it coated with the spice mix for a couple of minutes.

6. Combine tomatoes and cook on low heat for 5-6 minutes (stirring often) until vegetables have softened.
7. Add tofu back into the pan, cook while stirring occasionally for 3-4 minutes. Remove from flame. Stir half and half.
8. Enjoy with a side of brown rice.

6. Chili Veg Macaroni and Cheese

Time: 20 minutes
Ingredients (3 servings)

- 500 ml tomato soup
- 1 ½ medium onion (finely chopped)
- 1/ tsp paprika (smoked)
- ½ tsp red chili powder (adjust as per taste)
- ¼ tsp ground cumin
- 5 midsized mushrooms (sliced)
- 120 g cooked kidney beans
- Salt and pepper (as per taste)
- 1 bell pepper (sliced)
- 180 gm pasta (uncooked)
- ½ cup water
- 80 gm cheddar cheese (grated)
- Fresh spring onion and cilantro (chopped)

Method:

1. If you are using frozen soup, defrost in microwave for 12 minutes.
2. In the meantime, heat oil in a pan. Add peppers, onions, chili and finally, mushrooms.
3. Cook on low heat for a few minutes until the vegetables achieve a soft texture.

4. Add kidney beans and all spices. Season it well.
5. Add tomato soup, uncooked pasta along with water. Combine to simmer for 15-20 minutes. Stir regularly until pasta is nicely cooked. Add some more water if required.
6. Once ready, add half of the cheddar cheese to the pasta and combine. Top the pasta with remaining cheese and cook on low heat until the cheese melts into a golden brown.
7. Garnish with fresh cilantro, coriander, and spring onions. Serve hot with garlic bread or an accompaniment of your choice.

7. Chickpea Shakshuka

Time: 30 minutes
Ingredients (4-6 servings)

- 2 tbsp. olive oil
- ½ red bell pepper (chopped)
- ½ cup white onion (diced)
- 1 28-ounce can tomato puree
- 1 tbsp. maple syrup
- 1 ½ tsp smoked paprika
- 4 garlic cloves (chopped)
- 2 tsp ground cumin
- 3 tbsps. tomato paste
- 2 tsp chili powder
- ¼ tsp cinnamon (ground)
- 2 cups chickpeas (cooked and drained)
- Lemon slices
- Salt (as per taste)

Method:

1. Heat a big rimmed skillet over reduced/low heat. Slowly introduce olive oil, onion, garlic and bell pepper. Cook mixture for around 5-7 minutes, while stirring regularly. The mixture should be soft and aromatic.
2. Add tomato paste, maple syrup, tomato puree, salt, cumin, paprika, cinnamon powder, and cardamom. Mix well.
3. Simmer on low flame for 3-4 minutes stirring the mixture regularly. If you prefer a smoother and creamier texture, you may want to use a blender. However, you can leave it as it is if you prefer a more coarse result.
4. Add chickpeas and olives and stir the mixture to combine all ingredients well. Allow the flavors to blend, while simmering mixture for 15 minutes.
5. Adjust seasonings as required. For more smokiness, you can add more paprika. Similarly, if you want it sweeter, add more maple syrup.
6. Garnish with lemon juice, more olives and chopped greens (optional parsley or cilantro).
7. Serve with pasta, rice or bread. It can stay in the refrigerator for a maximum of 4 days, and frozen for a maximum of one month.

8. Black Bean Burger

Time: 25 Minutes
Ingredients (4 burger patties)

- 1 slice toasted and torn bread
- 1 ½ tsp fresh lime juice
- ½ tsp grated lime (rind)
- ½ walnut (chopped)
- 1/2 cup onion (chopped
- ¾ tsp cumin (ground)
- 1 can of unsalted black beans (wash and drain)
- ½ tsp hot sauce
- 1 ½ tbsps. garlic (chopped)
- 4 tsp olive oil
- 1 egg (beaten)
- Salt (as per taste)

Method:

1. Pulse bread in food processor 4-5 times before transferring to a large bowl.
2. Add onion, lime juice, salt, rind, beans, and garlic in processor. Pulse about 4-5 times.
3. Add bean mix, hot sauce, egg and walnut to the breadcrumbs.
4. Separate the mixture into equal parts and shape each one into a thick (3/4th inch) patty.
5. Heat oil in a pan and add patties. Cook evenly on slow heat for 7-8 minutes on each side until they achieve a brownish tinge.
6. Add sauces of your choice along with a slice of tomato and other raw veggies in burger buns to enjoy as delicious vegetarian burgers.

9. Potato - Mushroom Curry

Time: 20 Minutes
Ingredients (serves 4)

- 1 onion (chopped roughly)
- 1 big potato
- 1 large aubergine (chopped into tiny chunky pieces)
- 2 tbsps. oil
- 300 gm button mushrooms
- 200 ml vegetable stock
- 3-4 tbsps. curry paste
- Coriander (chopped)
- Salt
- 350 ml coconut milk

Method:

1. Add oil heating pan sufficiently. Introduce potato and roughly chopped onion. Cook covered for 5-10 minutes till your potatoes have softened.
2. Add mushrooms and chunks of aubergine and cook for 3-4 minutes.
3. Combine curry paste, coconut milk, and vegetable stock.
4. Boil mixture followed by simmering it on low heat for 10-12 minutes or till the potatoes get a soft texture.
5. Garnish with coriander and serve with rice, bread or naan.

10. Thai Red Vegetable Curry

Time: 25 Minutes
Ingredients (4 servings)

- 3 tbsps. olive oil
- 3 cloves garlic (minced)
- 1 large red bell pepper (sliced into strips)
- 1 tbsp. ginger (grated finely)
- 1 large yellow bell pepper (sliced into strips)
- 1 medium sized onion (chopped)
- Salt
- 1 ½ can coconut milk
- 3 carrots (peeled, sliced into ½ inch thick round pieces
- 2 tbsps. soy sauce
- 2 cups kale (thinly sliced)
- ½ cup water
- 2 tsp brown sugar
- 3 tbsps. Thai red curry paste
- Fresh basil or cilantro(chopped)
- Red pepper flakes (optional garnish)
- 3 tsp rice vinegar
- Sriracha/chili garlic sauce

Method:

1. Heat a large skillet. Introduce oil. Add onion and salt to cook until onion goes soft for 5-7 minutes. Keep stirring frequently.
2. Add garlic followed by ginger and cook for 2-3 minutes, while stirring continuously.
3. Add carrots and peppers and cook until peppers are slightly soft for 5 minutes while stirring continuously.

Combine flavorsome curry paste and mix nicely for 2-3 minutes.

4. Add coconut milk, kale, sugar, and water. Mix well. Simmer on slow heat. Cook until bell peppers and carrots become soft for 7-10 minutes. Stir frequently.

5. Remove from pot and season with vinegar, tamari or optional garnishing. Adjust salt as per taste.

6. Serve with a bed of rice.

Conclusion

Thanks for making it through to the end of *Vegetarian Recipes Cookbook.* Let's hope it was informative and provided you with all of the tools you need to achieve your goals, no matter what they may be.

The next step is to decide which of the tasty treats will be served first. All of them are easy to prepare with the simple guidelines provided. Why not start right now, and compile the list of everything you want to make in the first few days. You are sure to have the attention of your family when these yummy meals and snacks hit the kitchen and dining table.

With all of these new recipes, invite some friends over, and have a party. You are sure to be the hit of the neighborhood whether you choose breakfast, lunch or dinner for your menu planning. You could always have a few snacks to see if you have everyone's attention before you surprise them!

The Complete 5:2 Fast Diet Recipe Cookbook

Introduction

The following chapters will discuss all the recipes that you need to know to get started with the 5:2 diet. This diet plan is simple to follow. You have two days during the week that you fast and five days that you are allowed to feast (within reason). The idea is that with the two fast days, which should not be back to back, you can take in fewer calories and lose weight without all the work.

The hardest part about this diet plan is finding meals that are low enough in calories that you will not break the fast. Plus, you want them to be filling as well, so you aren't having to deal with all the temptation. This guidebook will provide you with many great meals for breakfast, lunch, dinner, and dessert that are all under 350 calories. This makes them easy to fit into your day, whether you are on a feast day or a fast day and can give you the results that you want! Take some time to look through the recipes and pick the ones you want to try out first!

There are plenty of books on this subject on the market, thanks again for choosing this one! Every effort was made to ensure it is full of as much useful information as possible. Please enjoy!

Chapter 1: Breakfast Recipes

Blueberry Compote and Yogurt

Calories: 75

What's in it

- Bran (1 tsp.)
- Fat-free yogurt (3 Tbsp.)
- Blueberries (50)

How's it done

1. Take out a bowl and place the blueberries inside. Place into the microwave and heat on a high setting for about 45 seconds so the blueberries will star tot burst.
2. Take the bowl out of the microwave and let them cool down a bit.
3. When the blueberries are done, top with the bran and the yogurt before serving.

Honey and Cottage Cheese Toast

Calories: 130

What's in it

- Honey (1 tsp.)
- Cottage cheese (2 Tbsp.)
- Bread (1 slice)

How's it done

1. Take the toast and place into the toaster, lightly toasting it to your preferences.
2. Spread out the cottage cheese on top of the bread slice and then drizzle on some honey before serving.

Swiss and Pear Omelet

Calories: 121

What's in it

- Shredded Swiss cheese (1.5 oz.)
- Almond milk (1.5 Tbsp.)
- Eggs (3)
- Salt (.25 tsp.)
- Chopped pear (.25)
- Diced shallot (1)
- Olive oil (1 Tbsp.)

How's it done

1. Heat up a skillet. When the skillet is warm, add in the salt, pear, and shallot and cook for five minutes.
2. While that is cooking, take out a bowl and whisk together the almond milk and the eggs. Pour this on top of the pears to cook.
3. Once you see that the edges are turning white and the bottom has started to cook, flip your omelet over.
4. Add the cheese to the middle and fold the omelet in half. Cook a bit longer to melt the cheese.

Chai Tea Smoothie

Calories: 123

What's in it

- Ice
- Stevia (.25 tsp.)
- Cinnamon (.25 tsp.)
- Vanilla yogurt (.25 c.)
- Banana (.5)
- Brewed chai tea (.5 c.)
- Almond milk (.5 c.)
- Flax meal (1 tsp.)

How's it done

1. To start, stir together the flax meal and the almond milk and let it stand for a bit while you work on the other ingredients.
2. Take out a blender and add the rest of the ingredients inside until smooth and creamy.
3. Add in some ice along with the almond milk mixture and blend some more. Sprinkle a little cinnamon on top and then serve.

Egg White Omelet

Calories: 78

What's in it

- Pepper
- Chopped chives (2)
- Grated courgetti (1)
- Diced tomato (1)
- Whisked egg whites (2)

How's it done

1. Take out a frying pan and let it heat up to low heat. Put the grill on high as well.
2. Add the egg whites to a bowl and season with the pepper before adding to the pan, swirling around so that it is spread out.
3. When the omelet bottom has started to cook, sprinkle in the chives, tomatoes, and courgetti and warm through for a few seconds.
4. Take this off the heat and place under the grill, making sure to leave the handle poking out of the oven. After another minute, it is time to enjoy.

Cheesy Scones

Calories: 162

What's in it

- Chopped bacon strips (3)
- Buttermilk (2 Tbsp.)
- Beaten egg (10 herbs (3 Tbsp.)
- Parmesan cheese (4 Tbsp.)
- Butter (75g)
- Self-rising flour (250g)

How's it done

1. Allow the oven to heat up to 420 degrees. Take out a skillet and cook your bacon until it is crisp, stirring along the way. Drain the bacon and keep it on a paper towel.
2. Sift the flour inside a bowl and add the butter. Mix with your hands until you get breadcrumbs. Add in the herbs and parmesan along with the bacon.
3. Beat the buttermilk and the eggs into a different bowl before adding into the breadcrumbs. Form this into a ball.
4. Place the dough onto a floured surface and shape into a round. Use a round cookie cutter to make circles of the dough.
5. Place these circles on a baking sheet and put into the oven. After 10 minutes, the scones should be done, and you can serve.

Breakfast in a Cup

Calories: 240

What's in it

- Watercress (1 handful for each plate)
- Olive oil
- Eggs (8)
- Cherry tomatoes (8)
- Slices of ham (4)
- Slices of bread (8)

How's it done

1. Turn on the oven and let it heat up to 340 degrees. Lightly oil up a muffin tin.
2. Take the bread and cut out little circles of them. Place one into each compartment of the muffin tin and push down to keep them in place.
3. Put the muffin tin into the oven and bake for ten minutes, so these become crisp. Take out of the oven and let cool down.
4. Divide up the ham between the 8 sections in the muffin tin and break an egg into each one. Put back into the oven.
5. This should cook for another 10 minutes so the egg can have time to set. Serve with some watercress and enjoy.

Pancakes

Calories: 285

What's in it

- Maple syrup (4 Tbsp.)
- Olive oil (3 Tbsp.)
- Skimmed milk (300ml)
- Egg (1)
- Buckwheat flour (50g)
- Wholemeal flour (50g)

How's it done

1. Sift both of your flours into a bowl to help them combine. In another bowl, beat the milk and egg together before adding in with the flours to make a batter.
2. Let this batter stand for about 30 minutes, so it has time to combine.
3. After this time, heat up some oil in a pan until it is hot, but not smoking. Add a few tablespoons of the batter and cook for a few minutes before flipping and cooking on the other side.
4. Move over to a plat and repeat this until you have eight pancakes. Serve two pancakes per person.

Autumn Spice Oatmeal

Calories: 265

What's in it

- Ginger (.25 tsp.)
- Cinnamon (.5 tsp.)
- Rolled oats (.5 c.)
- Asian pear (.5 c.)
- Almond milk (.66 c.)
- Apple juice (.33 c.)

How's it done

1. Take out your saucepan and place the pear, milk, and juice inside. Heat this on the stove until it is boiling.
2. Add in the rolled oats to this mixture and then turn the heat down to low. Cook all the ingredients together until done.
3. Sprinkle on the ginger and cinnamon and then serve warm.

Raspberry French Toast

Calories: 294

What's in it

- Orange slices (4)
- Vanilla (1 dash)
- Raspberries (100g)
- Butter (1 Tbsp.)
- Bread (8 slices)
- Skim milk (1.5 c.)
- Eggs (3)
- Cornflakes (2 c.)

How's it done

1. Add the cornflakes into a food processor and pulse a few times.
2. Take out a bowl and whisk together the milk and the eggs. When those are combined, add in the vanilla.
3. Soak the slices of bread inside the egg mixture and then coat with the cornflakes.
4. Take out your frying pan and melt the butter on top. Cook each slice of bread for a few minutes on both sides, so it becomes golden and crisp.
5. Serve with a twist of orange and some raspberries and enjoy.

Almond Butter Pudding

Calories: 290

What's in it

- Sliced apple (1)
- Coconut oil, melted (1 Tbsp.)
- Almond milk (2 Tbsp.)
- Salt
- Almond butter (2 Tbsp.)
- Chopped figs, dried (1)
- Chia seeds (1 Tbsp.)
- Chopped pear (1)
- Applesauce (.5 c.)

How's it done

1. Take out your blender and combine the pear and the applesauce until the mixture is smooth.
2. When that is done, add in the almond butter, fig, and chia seeds. Let this combine and then leave to set for 10 minutes or more.
3. After the ten minutes are up, add in the almond milk and the salt and blend some more until combined.
4. While the blender is still going, slowly drizzle in the coconut oil until it is all combined.
5. Serve this dip with the apple slices and enjoy.

Chapter 2: Lunch Recipes

Tomato Crispbreads

Calories: 112

What's in it

- Rye crispbreads (4)
- Green pepper, sliced (1)
- Balsamic vinegar (1 tsp.)
- Chopped parsley (2 Tbsp.)
- Grated and juiced lime (1)
- Red chili, diced (1)
- Diced cherry tomatoes (8)

How's it done

1. Mix together all of your ingredients besides the crispbreads until well combined.
2. Let these ingredients set for about ten minutes.
3. When the time is up, serve on top of the crispbread and then serve.

Asian Salad

Calories; 140

What's in it

- Pepper
- Salt
- Bean sprouts (.5 c.)
- Romaine lettuce (1 c.)
- Bok choy (1 c.)
- Chopped apple (.5)
- Chopped cucumber (.5 c.)
- Water (1 Tbsp.)
- Balsamic vinegar (1 Tbsp.)
- Sesame oil (1 tsp.)
- Chopped broccoli (.5 c.)

How's it done

1. Add a cup of water to a pan and let it come to a boil. Add in the broccoli and cook it for a few minutes. When the broccoli is done, add it to a bowl of ice water to help stop the cooking process.
2. Place the water, balsamic vinegar, and sesame oil into a bowl and whisk them together.
3. Now add in the greens, apple, cucumber, and broccoli to the bowl. Top with the sprouts and season with some pepper and salt before serving.

Spinach and Garlic Mushrooms

Calories: 135

What's in it

- Pepper
- Baby spinach (100g)
- Lemon rind (1)
- Garlic and herb cream cheese (100g)
- Water (4 Tbsp.)
- Mushrooms (4)

How's it done

1. Add the water into a frying pan and heat it up. Add in the mushrooms and let them heat until they are soft.
2. While the mushrooms are cooking, mix together the rind and the cream cheese and then divide up the mushrooms. Place the lid on top and cook for five minutes.
3. Take the lid off and add the spinach in with the mushrooms. Put the lid back on and cook a bit longer. Serve when ready.

Melon-Ginger Soup

Calories: 80

What's in it

- Mint leaves
- Nutmeg (1 tsp.)
- Milk (.25 c.)
- Honey (1 Tbsp.)
- Salt
- Lime juice (.5)
- Grated ginger (1.5 tsp.)
- Cubed cantaloupe (1)

How's it done

1. Take out the blender and add in all the ingredients besides the mint leaves and the milk inside. Blend these together until smooth.
2. Now add in the milk and blend a bit more. Garnish with the mint leaf and then serve.

Zucchini Pizzas

Calories: 210

What's in it

- Salt
- Italian seasoning (1 tsp.)
- Mozzarella (.25 c.)
- Marinara sauce (2 Tbsp.)
- Olive oil (1 tsp.)
- Sliced zucchini (1)

How's it done

1. Allow the oven to heat up to 350 degrees. Line a baking sheet with some parchment paper.
2. Take out a bowl and toss the oil with the zucchini slices. Add these to the baking sheet and top with some marinara sauce, cheese, Italian seasoning, and salt.
3. Place in the oven to bake for 15 minutes and then serve.

Peaches and Brie Quesadilla

Calories: 225

What's in it

- Grated lime rind (1 tsp.)
- Lime juice (2 Tbsp.)
- Honey (2 Tbsp.)
- Flour tortillas (2)
- Brie cheese (3 oz.)
- Brown sugar (1 tsp.)
- Chopped chives (1 Tbsp.)
- Sliced peaches (1 c.)

How's it done

1. Take out a bowl and add in the brown sugar, chives, and peaches. Toss everything around to coat.
2. Spread half of each tortilla with half the brie and half the peaches. Fold this in half and add to a hot skillet.
3. Cook these for a few minutes on each side to brown them a bit. Take out of the skillet and keep warm.
4. Take out another bowl and whisk together the lime rind, lime juices, and honey. Serve this with the quesadillas.

Turkey Burgers

Calories: 217

What's in it

- Salsa
- Crisp lettuce
- Zest and juice from a lemon (.5)
- Olive oil (1 Tbsp.)
- Diced red onion (.5)
- Grain mustard (.5 tsp.)
- Cubed apple (1)
- Diced beetroots (4)
- Burgers
- Pepper
- Salt
- Lemon juice (.5)
- Diced sweet red onion (.5)
- Thyme (2 tsp.)
- Lean turkey mince (450g)

How's it done

1. Take out a bowl and mix together the turkey, lemon juice, chopped onion, and thyme. Shape this into four patties.
2. Take out another bowl and mix together all the ingredients for the salsa and set aside.
3. Turn on the grill and let it have time to heat up. Cook the burgers on each side for about 6 minutes.
4. Serve one burger per person and add in the lettuce for garnish and the salsa.

Gazpacho Soup

Calories: 176

What's in it

- Green and red pepper, diced (.5 each)
- Chopped scallions (2)
- Pepper
- Salt
- Sherry vinegar (2 Tbsp.)
- Olive oil (1 Tbsp.)
- Cubed cucumber (.5)
- Garlic cloves (3)
- Chopped scallions (4)
- Tomatoes (2.2 lbs.)

How's it done

1. Put the cucumber, garlic, scallions, and tomatoes into a blender and let them pulse until smooth.
2. Push this mixture through a sieve a few times to help get rid of the skins and the pulps.
3. Put it back into the blender and slowly add in the sherry vinegar and the olive oil. Season this and place into the fridge to chill for a little bit.
4. Serve with some scallions and diced peppers on top.

Thai Crab Cakes

Calories 224

What's in it

- Vegetable oil (1 tbsp.)
- Lemon juice (.5)
- Scallions chopped (4)
- Chopped coriander (1 handful)
- Diced red chili (1)
- Breadcrumbs (5 oz.)
- Beaten eggs (2)
- Mashed potato, cold (8 oz.0
- Canned crabmeat (12 oz.)
- Dip
- Brown sugar (1 tsp.)
- Lime juice (.5)
- Garlic clove (1)
- Soy sauce (3 Tbsp.)

How's it done

1. Take out a bowl and mix all of the ingredients for the dip together until well combined. Set this to the side.
2. Now take out another pan and mix together half the beaten egg with the lemon juice, chili, scallions, coriander, potatoes, and crabmeat.
3. Form this into 12 cakes and dust with flour. Dip this into the remainder of the beaten egg and then into the breadcrumbs.
4. Heat up some oil in a frying pan and then add in the cakes. Fry these for the next ten minutes, making sure to flip over.

5. After this time, take the cakes out of the skillet, drain on some paper towels, and then serve with some of your dipping sauce.

Pecan and Strawberry Salad

Calories: 203

What's in it

- Soft goat cheese (1 Tbsp.)
- Macadamia oil (1 tsp.)
- Balsamic vinegar (1 Tbsp.)
- Honey (1 tsp.)
- Chopped pecans (1 Tbsp.)
- Halved strawberries (1 c.)
- Baby spinach (2.5 c.)

How's it done

1. Take out a large bowl and whisk together the oil, balsamic vinegar, and honey. Add in a bit of water if it is too thick.
2. Add the spinach into the bowl and toss it with the other ingredients. Let this soak in for the next ten minutes.
3. When ready to serve, stir the spinach around again and top with the goat cheese, pecans, and strawberries.

Chapter 3: Dinner Recipes

Oriental Chicken

Calories: 157

What's in it

- Chopped ginger (4 slices)
- Soy sauce (2 tsp.)
- Pak choi (1 head)
- Sliced button mushrooms (4)
- Chicken breast (120g)

How's it done

1. It is best to use a steamer basket to do this. Take a plate and put the pak choi on it, followed with some soy sauce, the ginger, the mushrooms, and then the chicken on top.
2. Place these into the steamer and let them steam for ten minutes, or until the chicken is tender and done.
3. Divide up into two portions and serve.

Lemony Cod

Calories: 98

What's in it

- Pepper
- Balsamic vinegar (1 Tbsp.)
- Cherry tomatoes (6)
- Stalk of mint, chopped (1)
- Lemon juice and rind (1)
- Cod fillet (65g)

How's it done

1. Allow the oven time to heat up to 320 degrees. Tear off enough foil to cover the fish up.
2. Add the fish to the foil and then squeeze some lemon juice on top along with the zest and the mint. Fold up the foil to make sure that juices don't come out.
3. Place the tomatoes and vinegar on the fish as well and put into the oven to bake.
4. After 12 minutes, the fish should be cooked through, and you can take it out of the oven to cool before serving.

Vegetable Chow Mein

Calories: 143

What's in it

- Lime (.5)
- Shirataki noodles (150g)
- Oyster sauce (1 Tbsp.)
- Rice wine vinegar (1 Tbsp.)
- Soy sauce (1 Tbsp.)
- Sliced carrot (1)
- Chopped broccoli (125g)
- Sliced red pepper (1)
- Sliced mushrooms (125g)
- Vegetable oil (1 Tbsp.)

How's it done

1. Take a look at the package directions to see how to cook up the noodles. When they are done, set them aside.
2. Take out your frying pan and heat up the oil inside. Add in the prepared vegetables and let them cook for three minutes. Add these in with the noodles.
3. Top this mixture with the oyster sauce, vinegar, and soy sauce. Divide into two portions and serve with the lime squeezed on top.

Shrimp Cocktail

Calories: 95

What's in it

- Pineapple ring (1)
- Cayenne pepper (2 pinches)
- Shredded lettuce leaves (4)
- Mayo (1 Tbsp.)
- Sweet chili sauce (2 tsp.)
- Shelled shrimp (10)

How's it done

1. Take out a small bowl and mix together the sweet chili and the mayo to make your dressing.
2. Place the lettuce at the bottom of two bowls.
3. In another bowl, combine the pineapple pieces with the shrimp. Divide this between the two dishes with the lettuce.
4. Top with the dressing and some paprika and cayenne before serving.

Provencale Beef Bake

Calories: 123

What's in it

- Italian herbs (2 tsp.)
- Sliced garlic cloves (2)
- Diced aubergine (1)
- Chopped tomatoes (240g can)
- Ground beef (60g)

How's it done

1. Allow the oven time to heat up to 320 degrees. While that is heating up, fry up the ground beef with the garlic until it is done. Drain off the extra fat.
2. Add in the aubergines and fry for a bit longer. Mix in the mixed herbs and the tomatoes.
3. Pour this mixture into a baking dish and place into the oven. After ten minutes, you can take it out and allow to cool.
4. Divide between two plates and serve.

Veggie Quiches

Calories: 185

What's in it

- Liquid egg replacer (1 carton)
- Monterey Jack cheese (.75 c.)
- Corn kernels (.5 c.)
- Water chestnuts (.25 c.)
- Broccoli florets (1.5 c.)
- Parmesan cheese (2 Tbsp.)
- Crumbled crackers (6)

How's it done

1. Allow the oven to heat up to 350 degrees. Take out a muffin tin and lightly oil them up.
2. Add the parmesan and the cracker crumbs into a small bowl. Boil our broccoli for a few minutes before draining and chopping up.
3. Add the cheese, corn, cracker mixture, water chestnuts, and broccoli into each muffin cup. Pour on the egg replacer on top.
4. Add these to the oven and bake for 20 minutes or until done. Allow them to stand for a few minutes before serving.

Vegetable Chili

Calories: 220

What's in it

- Water
- Brown rice (5 oz.)
- Sour cream to serve
- Green beans (5 oz.)
- Kidney beans (14 oz.)
- Chopped tomatoes (14 oz.)
- Sliced mushrooms (8 oz.)
- Ground cumin (2 tsp.)
- Olive oil (1 Tbsp.)
- Chopped red chilies (2)
- Crushed garlic cloves (2)

How's it done

1. Cook up the rice using the instructions on the bag. Drain the water out and keep the rice warm.
2. Fry up the chili and the garlic with some oil for a few minutes before adding the mushrooms and cumin. Cook for a few more minutes.
3. Add in the kidney beans, tomatoes, and a little water. Stir and simmer this for another 10 minutes.
4. Finally, add in the green beans and cook for another 5 minutes to let the sauce thicken.
5. Divide this mixture between four bowls and serve with a quarter of the rice along with some sour cream on each one.

Tofu Wraps

Calories: 183

What's in it

- Tofu (.25 package)
- Diced plum (1)
- Lime juice (1 tsp.)
- Olive oil (1 tsp.)
- Coconut aminos (1 tsp.)
- Salt
- White pepper
- Romaine lettuce (1 leaf)
- Sprouts (.25 c.)
- Diced cucumber (2 Tbsp>)
- Grated carrot (2 Tbsp.)

How's it done

1. Take out a bowl and whisk together the lime juice, olive oil, and aminos. Add the plum and smoosh it into the sauce.
2. Crumble the tofu into the bowl and add in the cucumber and carrot. Let these ingredients marinate together for at least ten minutes.
3. Wrap these ingredients in a lettuce leaf and serve with the sprouts.

Dinner Tostada

Calories: 205

What's in it

- Guacamole (1 Tbsp.)
- Sour cream (1 Tbsp.)
- Black olives
- Chopped tomato (2 Tbsp.)
- Chopped lettuce (.5 c.)
- Shredded cheese (2 Tbsp.)
- White corn tortilla (1)
- Refried beans (3 Tbsp.)

How's it done

1. Lay out the tortillas and spread the beans out on top. Top this with some cheese.
2. Allow the oven to heat up to 350 degrees. Lay the tortilla on a baking sheet and place into the oven to bake or a few minutes.
3. Top this with the guacamole, sour cream, black olives, tomato, and lettuce before serving.

Sweet Potato Bowl

Calories: 215

What's in it

- Drained black beans (.25 c.)
- Cottage cheese (.25 c.)
- Low-calorie dressing (1 Tbsp.)
- Chopped salad greens (1.5 c.)
- Sliced sweet potato

How's it done

1. Take out a pot and add two cups of water inside. Add in the slices of sweet potato and reduce the heat a little bit.
2. Allow these to cook for the next ten minutes. Drain out the water when the time is up.
3. Place the greens into a bowl with the dressing and fluff them up while combining. Add the sweet potatoes in and top with the black beans and cottage cheese before serving.

Tuna Tacos

Calories: 254

What's in it

- Vegetable oil (1 Tbsp.)
- Taco seasoning mix (1 Tbsp.)
- Chipotle peppers (1 tsp.)
- Chopped cilantro (3 Tbsp.)
- Sour cream (.33 c.)
- Chopped green onions (1 c.)
- Shredded purple cabbage (2 c.)
- Tuna steak (8 oz.)
- Taco shells, hard (4)

How's it done

1. To start this recipe, take out a bowl and combine the chipotle peppers, cilantro, sour cream, and green onions.
2. Place the tuna into a bowl and add on the taco seasoning mix. Heat up some oil in a pan before adding in the tuna steak. Cover and let it cook until it reaches the desired doneness.
3. Turn the heat down a bit and add in the sour cream mixture. Cook so that it is warmed up, but do not let these ingredients start boiling.
4. Add the shells to the microwave and let them heat up for 20 seconds. Add the tuna and sour cream to the mixture.
5. Top with the purple cabbage before serving.

Spaghetti Rustico

Calories: 292

What's in it

- Basil (1 handful)
- Pepper
- Chopped black olives (2 oz.)
- Chopped capers (1 Tbsp.)
- Chopped tomatoes (14 oz.)
- Anchovy fillets, chopped (4)
- Chili flakes, dried
- Crushed garlic clove (1)
- Olive oil (1 Tbsp.)
- Spaghetti (3.5 oz.)

How's it done

1. Start cooking up the spaghetti by following the instructions on the package.
2. During that time, heat up some oil in a pan and add in the anchovies, chili, and garlic. Cook for 4 minutes so that the anchovies begin to dissolve inside the mixture.
3. Add in the capers, olives, and tomatoes at this time before turning down the heat. Simmer for 20 minutes to help the sauce thicken.
4. Drain out the pasta and add it back to the pan. Stir in the sauce and the fresh basil. Serve warm.

Chapter 4: Dessert Recipes

Fruit Salad

Calories: 50

What's in it

- Raspberries (.25 c.)
- Blueberries (.25 c.)
- Cubed pineapple (.33 c.)
- Sliced strawberries (.25 c.)
- Cubed watermelon (1 c.)
- Cubed cantaloupe (1 c.)

How's it done

1. Start by preparing all the fruits and cutting into small pieces.
2. Mix the fruit together and keep in the fridge for when you are ready to eat.

Baked Pears

Calories: 50

What's in it

- Brown sugar (.25 tsp.)
- Lemon juice (1 tsp.)
- Cinnamon (.5 tsp.)
- Tart jam (1 tsp.)
- Pear (1)

How's it done

1. Allow the oven to heat up to 350 degrees. Take out a baking dish and spray with some cooking spray.
2. Cut your pear in half and scoop out the seeds and the core, allowing a small well to be in the middle of both halves. Place this into your baking dish.
3. Sprinkle a bit of lemon juice on each pear half and top with the cinnamon and brown sugar.
4. Add in a bit of the jam into each half and then put the whole baking pan into the oven. Bake this for 20 minutes until tender.

Berry Parfait

Calories: 50

What's in it

- Granola (1 tsp.)
- Greek yogurt, plain (2 Tbsp.)
- Raspberries (.25 c.)
- Sliced strawberries (.25 c.)

How's it done

1. Inside a small bowl, mix the raspberries and the strawberries together.
2. Place the yogurt into your serving bowl and then place the fruit on top. Sprinkle with the granola and serve.

Blueberry Muffins

Calories: 93

What's in it

- Blueberries (1 c.)
- Applesauce (1 Tbsp.)
- Brown sugar (.25 c.)
- Greek yogurt (.5 c.)
- Egg white (1)
- Salt (.25 tsp.)
- Baking powder (1 tsp.)
- Whole wheat flour (.75 c.)

How's it done

1. Allow the oven to heat up to 375 degrees. Take out a muffin tin that can make six muffins and spray with some oil.
2. In a bowl, mix together the salt, baking powder, and flour. In a second bowl, whisk together the applesauce, brown sugar, yogurt, and egg white.
3. When these are done, slowly pour the wet ingredients in with the flour mixture and slowly combine. Then add in the blueberries.
4. Spoon this batter into the muffin cups, leaving a little room at the top for the batter to expand.
5. Place into the oven to bake. After 15 minutes, the muffins should be done, and you can take them out of the oven.
6. Allow some time to cool before serving.

Strawberry Granola

Calories: 91

What's in it

- Water (1 Tbsp.)
- Vanilla (1 tsp.)
- Flaxseed oil (3 Tbsp.)
- Agave nectar (.25 c.)
- Dried strawberries (2 c.)
- Wheat germ (.5 c.)
- Oats (2 c.)

How's it done

1. Allow the oven to heat up to 275 degrees. Take out a medium bowl and stir together the wheat germ and the oats.
2. Now take out a pan and heat up the water, vanilla, flaxseed oil, and agave nectar on low heat. Bring this to a simmer, but do not let it boil.
3. Pour this mixture on top of the oat mixture and stir around.
4. Bring out a baking tray and coat it with some oil. Add the oat mixture and spread it around before placing into the oven.
5. After 30 minutes, you can add the strawberries on and sir the granola a little bit. Bake for another 15 minutes before allowing to cool down and serve.

Bread Pudding

Calories: 125

What's in it

- Vanilla (1 tsp.)
- Ground cinnamon (1 tsp.)
- Brown sugar (.25 c.)
- Raisins (.25 c.)
- Milk (2 c.)
- Egg whites (8)
- Applesauce (2 Tbsp.)
- Whole wheat bread (6 slices)

How's it done

1. Allow the oven time to heat up to 350 degrees. Use some cooking spray to prepare a baking dish.
2. Tear up the bread and place into the bottom of the baking dish.
3. Take out a bowl and whisk together the milk, egg whites, and applesauce. Then stir in the vanilla, cinnamon, sugar, and raisins.
4. Pour this on top of the bread. Use a fork to press the bread into the liquid and then place into the oven to bake.
5. After 45 minutes, the bread will be nice and browned, and you can take out of the oven. Allow some time to cool and then enjoy.

Apple Crisp

Calories: 155

What's in it

- Granola (.25 c.)
- Agave nectar (4 tsp.)
- Lemon peel, grated (1 tsp.)
- Plain Greek yogurt (2 Tbsp.)
- Cinnamon
- Ginger (.25 tsp.)
- Brown sugar (1 Tbsp.)
- Sliced apples (2)
- Coconut oil (1 Tbsp.)

How's it done

1. Take out a skillet and melt the coconut oil. Add in the apple slices to the hot skillet and cook for a few minutes.
2. Now add in the cinnamon, ginger, and sugar and keep cooking until your apples are cooked.
3. While you are apples are cooking, take out a bowl and combine the yogurt and lemon peel together. Whip these until they are light and fluffy.
4. When your apples are done, divide that mixture between four bowls. Top with half a tablespoon of the whipped yogurt and a bit of agave nectar.
5. Sprinkle the granola on top and enjoy.

French Toast Waffles

Calories: 256

What's in it

- Bread slices (4)
- Ground nutmeg
- Cinnamon (.5 tsp.)
- Vanilla (1 tsp.)
- Sugar (1 Tbsp.)
- Milk (.5 c.)
- Beaten eggs (2)

How's it done

1. Take out your waffle iron and spray it with some cooking spray before heating up.
2. In a bowl, whisk together the nutmeg, cinnamon, vanilla, sugar, milk, and eggs together until blended.
3. Dip your bread into this batter, making sure that you coat both sides.
4. Place the bread slice into your waffle iron and cook for about 7 minutes until it is golden brown. Continue until all the bread is done and then serve.

Apple Fritter

Calories: 252

What's in it

- Lemon juice (2 Tbsp.)
- Powdered sugar (.5 c.)
- Chopped apple (.5 c.)
- Egg (1)
- Cinnamon (.5 tsp.)
- All-purpose flour (.5 c.)
- Whole wheat flour (.25 c.)
- Salt
- Sugar (2 Tbsp.)
- Sliced margarine (2 Tbsp.)
- Warm water (1.5 Tbsp.)
- Active dry yeast (.25 package)
- Mil (.25 c.)

How's it done

1. Heat up the milk in a skillet until it is scalding. While the milk is heating up, add the yeast to the warm water and let it froth for five minutes.
2. In a bowl, stir together the salt, sugar, and margarine. When this is done, pour the hot milk in and let the margarine start to melt. Stir in the whole wheat flour, egg, cinnamon, and yeast mixture and stir until blended.
3. Now add in the all-purpose flour and form the mixture into a dough. Turn this onto the counter and knead for a few minutes.
4. Add some oil to a mixing bowl before adding in the dough. Cover with a clean cloth and let it rise for 90 minutes.

5. When this is done, punch it down and then knead in the prepared apples. Divide into four portions and form each part into a sphere.
6. Place these onto a baking sheet and let them rise for an hour.
7. Allow the oven to heat to 350 degrees. Place the baking pan in the oven and let these bake for the next 15 minutes.
8. While the dough is baking, mix together the lemon juice and powdered sugar to make a glaze.
9. Take the fritters out of the oven and brush on the glaze as they cool down.

Conclusion

Thank you for making it through to the end of this book, let's hope it was informative and able to provide you with all of the tools you need to achieve your goals whatever they may be.

The next step is to get started on 5:2 diet plan. This diet plan is meant to fit around your schedule and to help you lose the weight that you want, without having to follow complicated formulas or having to count each and every calorie that you consume. Many people find that this can be a simple diet plan to follow once they get used to the schedule and when they can find the perfect recipes to help with the feast and the fast days.

Go ahead and try the recipes in this book.

** Remember to use your link to claim your 3 FREE Cookbooks on Health, Fitness & Dieting Instantly

https://bit.ly/2OazEZu

Printed in Great Britain
by Amazon

59070615R00112